bankruptcy
do it yourself

Attorney Janice Kosel

Edited by Ralph Warner

NOLO PRESS, 950 Parker St., Berkeley, CA 94710

Printing History

Nolo Press is committed to keeping its books up-to-date. Each new printing, whether or not it is called a new edition, has been completely revised to reflect the latest law changes. If you are using this book any considerable time after the last date listed below, be particularly careful not to rely on information without checking it.

First Edition	September 1980
Second Edition	January 1983
Second Printing	July 1983
Third Edition	January 1984
Second Printing	July 1984

ISBN 0-917316-76-2
©copyright 1984 by Janice Kosel

To Elsie and Otto
with love

ACKNOWLEDGMENTS

Thanks to:

Jake Warner

Nancy Carol Carter and Joyce Saltalamachia of the law library at
  Golden Gate University, San Francisco, California

Elizabeth Greene and her fine secretarial staff: Margaret Chew, Chris
  Chimera, Judy Chiu, Ginger Crader, Lanny Laub, Portia Stewart
  and Amy Sukoff

Peter Honigsberg, Dave Brown and Judith Sagal (an attorney in
  Richmond, California)

Two anonymous friends for the gifts of their practical insight and
  experience

TO OUR READERS

This book can be of great help to you and your family. The advice about bankruptcy is as sound as I can make it, after much study of, and experience in, the area. Many knowledgeable people have reviewed these materials, and I have included many of their suggestions for change and clarification. But advice will not always work. Like well-meaning recommendations of all kinds, some of the advice I present here may not be helpful. So here are some qualifications. If you have access to a lawyer's advice and it is contrary to that given here, follow your lawyer's advice; the individual characteristics of your problem can better be considered by someone in possession of all the facts. Laws and procedures vary considerably from one state to the next and it is impossible to guarantee that every bit of information and advice contained here will be accurate. It is your responsibility to get a copy of your state exemption laws and bankruptcy rules and to make sure that the facts and general advice contained in this book are applicable in your state and to your situation.

● ● ● ● ● Bankruptcy rules and regulations are constantly changing and you will wish to check to be sure that information printed here is still current. And finally, please pay attention to this general disclaimer — of necessity, neither the author nor the publisher of this book makes any guarantees as to the uses to which this material is put. Thank you, and good luck!

ABOUT THE AUTHOR

Janice Kosel is a Professor of Law at Golden Gate University in San Francisco CA. She grew up in Berkeley and attended college and law school at the University of California. Janice practiced law in San Francisco for several years before she began teaching law school in 1974.

ABOUT NOLO PRESS

This book was created by Nolo Press in Berkeley CA. Nolo Press consists of a group of friends (some lawyers, some not) who have come to see much of what passes for the practice of law as meaningless mumbo jumbo and needless paper shuffling designed by lawyers to mystify and confuse. Since 1971 Nolo has published more than a dozen books designed to give ordinary people access to their legal system, and, in so doing, has become one of the principal energy centers of the self-help law movement.

CONTENTS

INTRODUCTION

Are you overburdened by debt?

Are you the victim of creditors' repeated phone calls, dunning letters, threats, repossession, or wage garnishment?

Are you unable or unwilling to pay all of your obligations?

If you answered yes to any of these questions, then this book is for you.

Here is what this book will do:

1. It will tell you what bankruptcy is all about and the effect it will have on you, your property, and your debts.
2. It will help you understand the different kinds of debts and how they are treated under the law.
3. It will explain how the law protects you against creditors and how one creditor may be able to collect from you whereas another may not.
4. It will help you decide whether you should file for bankruptcy.
5. Bankruptcy is only one of the legal solutions available to overburdened debtors. If you should decide against filing for bankruptcy, this book will point out other ways in which you can deal effectively with your creditors.
6. If you should decide to file for bankruptcy, this book will show you —step by step—how to do it yourself. Personal bankruptcies often are not very difficult—perhaps no more so than preparing your own income tax return.
7. The law is sometimes a little tricky or technical in its treatment of particular types of debts or property. This book will alert you to those problem areas and point out when you should consult a lawyer. It will also help you understand and deal with your lawyer more effectively.

To get the most out of this book, you must become an active participant. So try to put aside your anxieties for awhile. Read the whole book over once before you make any decisions. Then get to work. Start a file. Collect all your bills. Fill out the worksheets. Then decide on a sensible solution to your financial problems. And follow through with that decision.

THE EMOTIONAL SIDE OF BANKRUPTCY

The odds are, if you are looking through this book, that you are mighty worried. It's not easy to cope with financial troubles. Feelings of anger, disbelief, helplessness, despair, guilt, shame, anxiety, confusion, frustration—all are commonly aroused by debt problems. Unfortunately, these kinds of negative feelings are often exacerbated by a feeling of isolation—a perception that you may be the only one with these kinds of problems. But you are not alone!

Recent studies indicate that more and more people are becoming overburdened with debt. Perhaps they bought too much on credit, egged on by advertising campaigns that encourage people to buy whether they need the item or not. Or they are pushed over the brink by unexpected events—a family breakup, illness, layoff from a job, a new baby. Still others have simply lost ground, inch by inch, to the ravages of inflation.

Whatever the underlying causes, record numbers of personal bankruptcies have been filed in recent years. Over the last three decades, the number of bankruptcies has risen over 2000 percent. Now over half a million bankruptcy petitions are filed annually. So if you are suffering financial difficulties, you are not alone. Like former president Ulysses S. Grant, football great Craig Morton, and many others, you may find that the answer to your money problems lies in a declaration of bankruptcy.

Unfortunately, most people don't know very much about bankruptcy. They can be made to feel guilty or ashamed even though the idea of getting a fresh start free of debt is a tradition of long legal and moral standing. Indeed, the foundation of bankruptcy is in large part

every creditor shall release what he has lent to his brother . . . . .

biblical. In Deuteronomy (15:1-2), it is stated that "At the end of every seven years you shall grant a release and this is the manner of the release: every creditor shall release what he has lent to his neighbor; he shall not exact it of his neighbor, his brother, because the Lord's release has been proclaimed." That's bankruptcy in a nutshell—a forgiveness of debt, available to each and every one of us every six years.

THE EMOTIONAL SIDE OF BANKRUPTCY

Although the actual law of bankruptcy had its origin in ancient Rome, its American roots are firmly entrenched. A national bankruptcy law was contemplated over two hundred years ago by our founding fathers in the Constitution and was first enacted in 1800. In 1978, Congress made major revisions in the bankruptcy law because it had become apparent over the years that the old law did not provide adequate relief for consumer debtors. Perhaps now, more and more people will exercise the valuable legal right to declare bankruptcy, make a fresh start, and free themselves from creditor harassment and the worries and pressures of too much debt.

Unfortunately, many myths have grown up around bankruptcy. For example, many people worry that they will lose their jobs or the right to vote if they declare bankruptcy. They won't. Indeed, their employers, friends, and neighbors probably will not even know about the bankruptcy. Although bankruptcy is a matter of public record, most people have better things to do than follow bankruptcy filings in the legal newspapers or search through court records.

Other people fear that their credit ratings will be ruined if they file for bankruptcy. But if a person is considering bankruptcy, his or her credit rating is probably not very good anyway. In fact, one's credit rating sometimes actually improves with bankruptcy because of the elimination of old debts. The re-establishment of a perfect credit rating won't happen overnight, but that's not the end of the world. Remember what got you into trouble in the first place—credit. Maybe you're better off without it for awhile.

It is important to realize that many thousands of people file for bankruptcy every year. This means that lots of people have managed to work their way through that very trying time just before and after bankruptcy. Listen to what a couple of them have to say.

Meet Gloria, a forty-five-year-old schoolteacher.

"Gloria, what caused you to declare bankruptcy?"

"I was recently divorced. I made the mistake of trying to live on the same income I had when I was married, and I couldn't do it. It wasn't there anymore. I went out and I didn't realize what I was doing. I was just signing my name.

"I have to take responsibility for my own share of negligence. But it's not all my fault. Creditors should be more careful about pushing all this money on people. Every time I paid off my debts, I got letters asking me to borrow more. They try to push credit on everybody. They want to get you hooked. They try to hook the weak people. I even asked some stores to close my account and they wouldn't do it. And if I didn't pay a two- or three-hundred dollar bill, they would just threaten to lower my limit from $1,500 to $1,200. Big deal. It was crazy. I just don't understand it."

"What was your financial situation like?"

"I was $8,000 in debt. I am a schoolteacher and my income then was about $16,000."

"Did you have to give up any of your property?"

"No. My only secured debt was the washing machine and my father paid that off for me so I could keep it."

"Was bankruptcy your last resort?"

"Yes. I tried a credit-counseling service first. It was free. I was amazed when I added up my bills. I found out I needed $650 a month minimum to pay my old bills. There was no way I could do that. It was a real worry. I didn't know what was going to happen."

"Did you consult a lawyer?"

"Yes, but it was still very frightening. I wasn't sure of the legal ramifications of anything. And I got the feeling the lawyer couldn't spare the time to explain everything to me—he sees so many people every day."

"Do you think you could have handled your own bankruptcy?"

"Yes. Now that I understand it I know that it's really pretty easy. But I was afraid when I started that I wouldn't have the expertise to do it myself. And then there's this—some people are real worriers and some are not. I am a worrier. Before I understood that bankruptcy was fairly simple, I was afraid that I was going to lie awake at night. I thought that I would rather pay a lawyer and get some peace of mind."

"How do you feel about going through bankruptcy?"

"I look at it as a personal failure, that I haven't managed that part of my life very well. I was embarrassed. I feel very bad about it. I had friends who thought it was horrible. It's a real stigma, just like divorce was a few years ago. I hated to admit it to people. Everyone is so uneducated about it. But still, it was something I had to do and I am glad I did. It was a little like facing up to a mistake and putting it behind me."

"Did any of your creditors contact you after bankruptcy?"

"Just my credit union. They tried to make me feel I had fraudulently gotten a loan—and I hadn't. They just couldn't believe they had made a mistake in loaning me money. They threatened to take me to court, but I knew they couldn't. When I tried to take out a second loan later, though, they told me I couldn't unless I paid the first one back. So I just decided not to borrow the money and I'm glad now that I don't have to pay it back."

"Did you have any difficulty re-establishing your credit after bankruptcy?"

"I was told it would be easy to get my credit back. Not true. It's really hard. But that was good. I have a tendency to spend every penny I have and right up to the credit limit.

"What I did was use my old credit cards — the ones I didn't owe money to. Pretty soon the other stores saw I had established credit. And in a few months they were doubling my limit and then doubling it again."

"What are your plans for the future?"

"My lawyer told me that a lot of his customers go through bankruptcy over and over again all through their lives. I vowed that I'd be different — if I ever get out of this, I'll never do it again. Now I have to live on a real close budget, and I use credit only when there is no alternative. If I get extravagant or forget what I am doing, I'll blow it. But I'm a survivor. I'm going to make it."

Bill, a thirty-four-year-old carpenter, shared many of Gloria's anxieties.

"What caused you to declare bankruptcy, Bill?"

"I had a good job in the construction industry; then I got laid off. I managed all right for awhile but then I got sick, and I didn't have any health insurance. You wouldn't believe the bills I ran up. When my doctor finally told me I could go back to work, I managed to find a job. And then one of my creditors got a judgment against me and garnished my paycheck. They just couldn't wait."

"What did you do?"

"I talked to a lawyer, but he said he couldn't do anything about the wage garnishment. It was too late. He suggested I go bankrupt."

"Did you file for bankruptcy?"

"Yes, but only after a lot of soul searching. Somehow I don't think it was really fair, but I didn't see any other way out. It was hard to lose part of my paycheck, but the biggest problem was that I knew my boss would eventually get angry about the wage garnishment hassle I was

5

putting him through and fire me. I couldn't let that happen."

"Did your lawyer handle your bankruptcy for you?"

"No. He wanted $350 to do it, and where was I going to get that kind of money? So I just did it myself. It wasn't nearly as difficult as I thought it would be.

"I bought the forms at a stationery store and filled them out. Lists of debts and lists of property. The woman at the public library helped me find some of the statutes I needed to know about. Then I took the papers to the clerk's office and they were very nice, very helpful. About a month later, I went to the meeting of creditors, and a couple of months after that to the court hearing. Everyone I dealt with was very polite. I felt kind of guilty, almost like a criminal. But that's not how they treated me at all. They were very nice."

"What happened after you filed for bankruptcy?"

"I started getting my whole paycheck again and that was great. My boss thanked me for getting the sheriff off his back. And I didn't hear from any of my creditors anymore. In fact, I didn't hear anything about my bankruptcy from anyone—ever. It was like it was my secret."

"How do you feel about going through bankruptcy?"

"I'm not proud of it, that's for sure. It was just something I had to do. It was either them or me.

"It's funny, though. I was afraid that trying to do my own bankruptcy might just add to my problems, but it didn't. Sure, I was pretty edgy and nervous about it, and a little afraid I'd make a mistake. But I also felt a certain sense of triumph and self-satisfaction out of doing it myself. It made me start feeling good about myself again. And boy did I ever need that!"

CHAPTER

2

$$$$$

LAWYERS

This book is not designed to replace lawyers. Rather, it is intended to give you an understanding of your legal situation when you fall behind in meeting your debts. That understanding is made up of a lot of different bits of information, and one of the most important is knowing whether or not you need a lawyer.

You don't automatically need a lawyer if you decide to file for bankruptcy. Many personal bankruptcies are straightforward, and you can represent yourself. If you decide to act as your own lawyer, you are said to be acting *in propia persona*, which is frequently shortened to *in pro per*. That's Latin for *you're on your own*. Sometimes it's not very comfortable being on your own, especially if your situation is a little complicated or unusual. Even after you read this book, you may feel a little nervous about handling your own bankruptcy. If so, don't lie awake at night worrying. Hire a lawyer. But don't stop reading — a thorough understanding of the rules and regulations relating to your debts will make you a lot better equipped to deal with both the lawyer and your personal situation during and after bankruptcy. In particular, you will know what you want a lawyer to do for you. You have a whole range of options.

1. You can simply consult with the lawyer and seek his or her advice. Sometimes this book will direct you to do exactly that when a particularly complex or confusing problem arises in your bankruptcy. Or you might consult a lawyer about whether bankruptcy makes sense for you, and if not, explore your alternatives.

   Part of a lawyer's job is to talk to people about these kinds of problems. You can hire a lawyer just to talk to you and nothing else. If that is what you decide to do, make sure the lawyer understands that all you want is a consultation. Then the lawyer will charge you only for the time he or she spends with you, perhaps $25 or $50. Be sure to check out in advance how much the lawyer will charge. Don't feel silly or awkward talking to lawyers about their fees. It's perfectly reasonable to do so.

2. If you want to be very cautious, you may choose to have a lawyer look at your completed bankruptcy forms to make sure you haven't

made a mistake. You should be able to find a lawyer to do this, but you may have to shop around a bit. Many lawyers won't give a layperson credit for being intelligent and will try to find fault with *anything* done *in pro per*. Be sure to find a lawyer who is willing to deal with you on your own terms. Again, check the hourly fee in advance.

3. Finally, you can hire a lawyer to handle your whole bankruptcy. If this is your decision, don't feel bad about it. Legal forms are often confusing — perhaps deliberately so to discourage people from solving their own problems without professional assistance.

BANKRUPTCY: DO IT YOURSELF

Finding a lawyer you can trust — and who also charges reasonable fees — is not an easy task. Unfortunately, most federally funded legal aid offices, which ordinarily will help people with low incomes without charge, will not handle bankruptcy cases because they are "fee generating." Roughly translated, this means that other lawyers object to Legal Aid handling a case for free when some lawyer could be making money at it.

If you don't know a good lawyer, see whether one of your friends does. This may be your best bet. If you must shop around, try the following:

1. *The local bar association's lawyer referral service.* They should be able to give you the names of a couple of lawyers who specialize in bankruptcy practice. Ask the referral service if the lawyers have been screened in advance for their expertise in bankruptcy — some bar associations don't do this. If they don't, you're just as well off with the yellow pages.
2. *A local consumer organization.* They may be able to recommend someone.
3. *Legal Aid.* Even if they won't handle your case, they may be able to direct you to someone who will.
4. *Ads.* Surveys have shown that many legal clinics that advertise heavily often don't charge the most reasonable prices. However, there are some attorneys who advertise who do deliver good services at good prices. One place to check advertisements is in the Lawyer Directory in the Nolo News where detailed price information is supplied (see order information at the front of this book).

REMEMBER: If you are shopping around, call several lawyers. Pick the one you feel most comfortable with, and agree on the charges before you make your appointment. If you want a consultation only, be careful of lawyers who want to take over your whole case for a fat fee. Never be intimidated into paying a lot when you have a good grasp of your situation and need only a little help.

CHAPTER

3

$$$$$

HOW DOES BANKRUPTCY WORK?

The results of bankruptcy are pretty simple. You get:

a fresh start
free of the burden of past debt
with enough of a grubstake to get you on your feet again

A SIMPLIFIED VIEW OF THE BANKRUPTCY PROCESS

Chapter 11 contains a complete check list of all the steps you must take to handle your own bankruptcy. Here is a brief overview of the procedure you will follow.

In order to file for bankruptcy, you must fill out the forms in Chapter 8 of this book. Take a look at them, but don't be intimidated. They are just lists of all your debts and all your property.

You can stop paying your debts the very day you take those forms, together with $60 in cash, to the bankruptcy clerk. You can also arrange for wage attachments and deductions from your paycheck for debts to your credit union to stop right away. But the legal mechanics aren't quite over yet.

About a month after you file your bankruptcy papers, you must go to the courthouse for a meeting with the *trustee*. He or she is the person in charge of your bankruptcy. It is the trustee's job to see if you have any property (called *nonexempt property*) that under the law must be turned over to your creditors. At that meeting, the trustee will ask you questions in order to determine which items (if any) of your property he or she can take.

12

HOW DOES BANKRUPTCY WORK?

A couple of months after that meeting, you must go to a court hearing. If you have been honest and truthful with your creditors and the trustee, the bankruptcy judge will tell you that he or she has already granted you a *discharge*—the formal forgiveness of all debt.

That's the general idea, all right, but like almost everything else, it does get a little more complicated. In all likelihood, you really won't be able to get rid of every one of your debts. But you probably will be able to keep all (or almost all) of your property. Why? Because the law divides all debt and property into various categories—and from a debtor's point of view, some categories are more favorable than others. In order to decide whether bankruptcy makes sense for you, you are going to have to master these categories. None of this is difficult, but some rules are going to be a little hard to understand the first time you

read them. So go slowly, and be prepared to read this material over a couple of times. And relax—we'll come back to the important rules again and again, and before you know it, they will seem almost like second nature to you. Just hang in there for now. And don't panic if, as you read on through the book, you forget what a word means. The important legal terms are all gathered together for easy reference in Chapter 12.

WHAT ARE DEBTS?

A *debt* is simply the legal obligation you have to pay someone money. Debts take a lot of different forms—rent, mortgage payments, taxes, bills, alimony, loans, installment payments, and court judgments are a few examples.

For the purposes of this book, we will want to divide all debts into two broad categories—debts that are dischargeable in bankruptcy and those that are nondischargeable in bankruptcy. A *dischargeable* debt disappears after bankruptcy—you are legally free not to repay it. Most debts are dischargeable. Typical examples include credit card purchases, rent, and medical bills.

A *nondischargeable* debt is not affected by bankruptcy—you must still repay it. This is the main exception to the general rule that bankruptcy will free you from past debt. As you just learned, probably only a few of your debts will be nondischargeable, but they can be important. Examples of the most important nondischargeable debts include student loans, alimony, and taxes. We'll talk more about nondischargeable debts in Chapter 5.

We will also want to divide debts into two other categories: unsecured and secured. A debt is *unsecured* if you never signed a written agreement pledging some of your property to the payment of that obligation. Most unsecured debts are dischargeable, so they disappear after bankruptcy. Typical examples include most credit card and charge account purchases, and personal loans from friends and relatives.

A *secured* debt is created when you make a written promise (usually in the form of a printed security agreement) that, if you do not pay, the creditor can take some particular item of your property—either the item you purchased or perhaps another item you pledged. Examples of merchandise where secured debts are common include motor vehicles, major appliances, expensive jewelry, and furniture. Most se-

14

cured debts are dischargeable in bankruptcy—that is, they will vanish after bankruptcy. But they are different from unsecured debts where there is no written security agreement. Sometimes, in exchange for wiping out a secured debt, you must either return the secured item to the creditor or, if you want to keep the item, pay for it.

Notice that I used the word *sometimes*. That means we'll have to divide secured debt into two types. In the first type, the secured creditor sold you the property or loaned you the money to buy it. If this is the case, you must be ready to lose the secured property in order to have the debt wiped out in bankruptcy—unless, of course, you want to pay for it. According to law, after bankruptcy you must pay the secured creditor either the amount of the debt or the present value of the property—whichever is less—in order to keep the property you pledged.

With the second type of secured debt, the secured creditor loaned you money and got you to pledge property that you already owned as security. You can get this debt wiped out and are free to keep the property after bankruptcy—without paying any more for it.

We'll talk more about secured debts and keeping or returning property in Chapters 5 and 10. For now, it's enough to know that there is a difference between most secured and unsecured debts.

WHAT IS PROPERTY?

Everything you own is *property*, including things you can reach out and touch, like your:

house
car
appliances
furniture
household goods
tools
sporting goods
clothes
jewelry
savings bonds
pets
cash in your pocket

and things you cannot touch, like your:

> bank account
> health and life insurance
> pension
> money other people owe you—like tax refunds, wages, insurance
> claims, and repayment on loans you made to others
> money you will receive on account of someone's death

After bankruptcy, you are entitled to keep only what is called *exempt* property. The federal and state governments have prepared lists of exempt property—things they think people need to get a fresh start. If an item is on the exempt list, you can keep it. Most people who are contemplating bankruptcy don't have a lot of property and are pleasantly surprised to find that they can keep most of it. Some examples of exempt property include equity[1] in your home or car, work tools, furniture, appliances, and clothes. Many types of exempt property are exempt only up to a certain dollar amount. We'll talk more about exempt property in Chapter 7.

If, on the very day you file for bankruptcy, you own any property with a significant monetary value that is not on the state or federal lists of exempt property, you lose it. Therefore, it is very important to plan for bankruptcy by selling all of your property that is not listed as exempt and using that money to buy something that is exempt. By doing so, you will be able to keep as much of your property as possible after bankruptcy.

The Final Twist: Even though an item of your property is listed as exempt, you may still lose it by going bankrupt if you pledged it as part of a secured debt that had to do with the purchase of the property. As you learned a few pages back, if you signed a security agreement on a particular piece of property at the time you bought it, you will have to pay the creditor either the amount of the debt or the present value of the item, whichever is less, in order to keep that property. If the secured debt had nothing to do with the original purchase or financing of the pledged property, you do not have to pay in order to keep it. Let us look at an example:

> Bruce is a plumber. He uses his pickup truck to get to four or
> five household jobs a day. Bruce borrowed money to buy his truck

and the creditor is listed on the pink slip. Bruce still owes $400 on the truck. Its present value, according to the want ads, is $750.

The truck is exempt property because it is necessary for Bruce's work. But the loan is a secured debt. In order for Bruce to keep the truck, he must pay the creditor $400, the amount of the debt.

Again, we'll talk about secured debts in Chapters 5 and 10 as well as how to keep the pledged or secured property. For now, just note that it may not always be possible to keep exempt property if it is the subject of a secured debt, unless you are willing to pay something more for it.

SOME QUESTIONS AND ANSWERS

People who are thinking about bankruptcy usually have a lot of questions. Here are some of the common ones:

Q: Do I have to be working in order to file for bankruptcy?

A: No. But most of the time it makes sense to delay bankruptcy until you are employed again. Bankruptcy gets rid of only those debts you have on the very day you file. If you are unemployed, you are probably still running up debts. Wait until you get a job and have some money coming in so that you have a real opportunity to make a fresh start.

Q: Will I lose my job if I go through bankruptcy?

A: It is unlikely that your boss will care if you declare bankruptcy — he or she may actually be relieved when you do so if your wages have been garnished. Governmental agencies are forbidden to fire you or deny you a license because of your bankruptcy. But there are some kinds of jobs that may be jeopardized by a declaration of bankruptcy — primarily work in which the employee must be bonded, like a jewelry clerk or a bank teller. If you have any worries about the effects of bankruptcy on your job, be sure to consult your employer before you file.

Q: Should my spouse and I both file for bankruptcy?

A: If you are married, it is usually best for you and your spouse to file

for bankruptcy, especially if each of you has incurred debts. You can both file on the same set of forms. But there are exceptions to this general rule — if your spouse had a lot of property before you were married and will not be able to convert all of it into exempt property, or if your spouse expects to receive money soon on account of someone's death, it may not be wise for both of you to file for bankruptcy. Consult an attorney about this.

Q: How long does bankruptcy take?

A: It usually takes only a couple of months from the day you file to the day you appear in court to be told that you have received your formal discharge from debt. But the most important date is the day you file. The court will notify your creditors so that collection efforts, repossessions, and wage garnishments will cease within a couple of days.

Q: Will bankruptcy be listed on my credit record?

A: Yes. Credit agencies are allowed to keep a notation of your bankruptcy on file for ten years. They list the total amount of dischargeable debts and specify which debts have been discharged in bankruptcy. It is up to individual creditors to decide what to do with that information.

Q: Will I lose everything if I go bankrupt?

A: No. In fact the majority of consumer debtors don't lose any of their property because it is exempt. If you have any secured debts, though, you may lose some property if you gave it as collateral when you bought that property—unless you pay either the amount of the debt or the value of the property, whichever is less. We'll talk more about this later.

Q: Will I be able to get rid of all my debts in bankruptcy?

A: Most debtors have some nondischargeable debts—like alimony or child support—that are not affected by bankruptcy. By shedding their other debts in bankruptcy, they are able to meet these obligations. If the bulk of your debts are nondischargeable, however, bankruptcy is probably not the best solution to your financial problems. We'll talk more about this in Chapter 4.

Q: How about debts cosigned by friends or relatives—what happens to them?

A: Bankruptcy protects only you. If a friend or relative cosigned your loan, he or she will have to pay it, even though you do not. You will not be legally required to reimburse your cosigning friend or relative if this happens; whether you do so is a matter between you and your conscience.

NOTES

1. *Equity* is your ownership interest in the property. It is calculated by subtracting the amount of any secured debts on the property from the present value of the property. For example, if a debtor has a car worth $2,000 and a secured debt against it of $1,500, the debtor's equity is $500 ($2,000-$1,500).

CHAPTER

4

$$$$$

SHOULD YOU FILE FOR BANKRUPTCY NOW?

Bankruptcy is a very powerful remedy for an overburdened debtor. It can be very tempting. But bankruptcy is not the solution to all of life's woes, nor is it the answer for everyone with money problems. Before you jump into it, give some careful thought to whether some less extreme measure might be more appropriate for you.

Oddly enough, it may turn out that you do not owe enough money to justify bankruptcy. It is a common mistake to file a bankruptcy petition when there is not enough need to do so. Bankruptcy is a drastic remedy. If you use it now, it will not be available to you again for another six years. The right to discharge from debt is a very valuable protection. Guard it jealously. Declare bankruptcy only when it will help you the most.

GENERAL GUIDELINES

There are a few rules of thumb to help you decide whether bankruptcy is a sensible solution to your money problems. It used to be said that it was not worthwhile to file for bankruptcy unless you could get rid of at least $2,000 in debts. Although bankruptcy is so much a product of each individual's circumstances that setting a monetary figure is likely to confuse more than clarify, I think that you would probably want to at least triple that figure today. But be very careful of any fixed amount —$6,000, $10,000, or even $20,000 of debt may be manageable for one family and an impossible burden for another. Therefore, a more

sensible way to decide whether you should file for bankruptcy requires looking at the percentage relationship your total debts bear to your yearly take-home pay. Generally, if all your outstanding debts total more than one-third of your annual take-home pay, you may want to consider bankruptcy. But before you draw any firm conclusions, you should figure out what your financial situation will be like after bankruptcy. Unless your income after bankruptcy will exceed your expenses, it is obvious that you will soon be in financial difficulties again, with another bankruptcy unavailable for six years. If this is your situation, you should probably delay bankruptcy until you get back on your feet. There is a worksheet in Chapter 6 that will help you decide if now is the right time to file, but before you fill it out you should read the rest of this chapter and Chapter 5.

SOME ALTERNATIVES TO BANKRUPTCY

If you decide after some study that bankruptcy isn't for you right now, what should you do? After all, you wouldn't have read this far if you weren't having debt problems. Above all, don't despair. Bankruptcy is not the only means of dealing with debts you are unable or unwilling to pay. There are a number of other options available to you, including the following:

1. Convert some, or all, of your assets into exempt property — that is, property that can't be taken by your creditors, even if they get a judgment against you and you don't declare bankruptcy. (Remember that unsecured creditors cannot take anything from you until they get a court judgment.) Most people can convert at least some of their property into exempt property. But you may not be able to protect all your assets. If you are working, some of your wages might not be exempt. If you have a secured debt, the creditors are free to repossess your property, even if it is an exempt asset, although they may have to go to court to do so. But if the rest of your property fits within your state (not the federal) exemption system, discussed in detail in Chapter 6, your creditors can't reach it, because each state legislature has decided that all debtors should be entitled to protect certain property from their creditors — whether or not they file for bankruptcy.

2. Negotiate directly with your creditors to extend the repayment period and/or reduce the amount of the debts.

3. File a Chapter 13 plan with the bankruptcy court that will free you from creditor harassment and allow you to keep all your property while you attempt to repay your debts in full or in part over a three-year period. This is perhaps the best alternative for debtors who have substantial nonexempt assets, large nondischargeable debts like student loans, debts cosigned by friends or relatives, or debts secured by property that the debtor wishes to retain but

cannot afford to pay off. If you think Chapter 13 might be the best solution to your financial problems, you will want to read *Chapter 13: The Federal Plan to Repay Your Debts.* See back of this book for order information.

4. **Consult with Consumer Credit Counselors to devise an overall repayment plan.** This is really just an informal Chapter 13 proceeding — without the legal protection — but in some situations it can work well. Consumer Credit Counselors is a nonprofit organization sponsored by creditors. They want you to repay your debts and think they will benefit in the long run by helping you figure out whether (and how) you can do it. Watch out for other so-called debt-counseling services. Many are really in the business of debt consolidation — getting you to trade in a lot of small debts for one big loan at a high rate of interest with either an impossible monthly payment or low monthly payments and one impossible payment at the end; that's when you lose your secured property! With debt consolidation outfits, it's easy to wind up worse off than you started.

BANKRUPTCY — WHETHER TO FILE OR TO WAIT

The material in this chapter may not answer all of your questions, but let's see whether we can clarify things with a few examples.

EXAMPLE 1: Lois retired in San Francisco with a modest income from a small pension and social security. She has an equity of $20,000 in her house, $1,000 in savings, $750 in U.S. savings bonds and a 1982 Buick sedan. She had an automobile accident while she was uninsured. Lois' car was only slightly damaged but the other car was totalled. A lawsuit has been filed against her for $10,000. What should Lois do?

Lois should consult a lawyer to represent her in the lawsuit. But she shouldn't be unduly concerned about the outcome. Because Lois has no current earnings, she can put all of her assets into property that is covered by California state exemptions — her home, food, clothes, household furniture and furnishings, jewelry, bank accounts to the extent they can be traced to her pension or social security, life insurance, etc. (see Chapter 4). If she does all this, it will all be safe from her creditors, regardless of how the lawsuit turns out. And, quite frankly, once the other lawyers figure out that they won't be able to collect anything from Lois, they'll probably start spending their energy elsewhere.

*   *   *

EXAMPLE 2: Frank has just finished a very messy divorce. He is flabbergasted at the result. He was ordered to pay his ex-wife $700 a month for spousal and child support and his take home pay is only $1,450 a month. Frank was left with his pension, his clothes and his pet cockatoo Pete. What should Frank do?

Frank is probably not in the right emotional frame of mind to seriously consider his financial situation. He has to simmer down. When he has cooled off, Frank needs to come up with a new budget for himself — and one item on that budget he is powerless to do anything about is his family support obligations. Those obligations are "nondischargeable" in both bankruptcy and Chapter 13 proceedings. Congress has decided that one of a person's most important creditors is his family. Obligations to them cannot be wiped out. It's a hard rule sometimes, but Frank is just going to have to cut back his lifestyle in order to make ends meet. If Frank is having difficulty meeting his other financial obligations, he might consider a trip to Consumer Credit Counselors and a Chapter 13 repayment plan. And, as a last resort, he might even consider selling Pete.

*   *   *

EXAMPLE 3: Alice is a waitress. She takes home about $600 (including tips) in a good month, but things have been slow lately. Alice doesn't have any money set aside because she's been having enough trouble just making ends meet. She lives in a small, nicely furnished apartment.

Alice is worried about one big bill — $3,000 she borrowed from a finance company for debt consolidation. She pledged all of her household furniture and furnishings as security for the repayment of the loan. Now Alice is having difficulty making the monthly payments and is afraid she'll lose her household goods. What should Alice do?

BANKRUPTCY: DO IT YOURSELF

The finance company really isn't going to come and take away Alice's furniture. They may threaten to do so, but they won't. Why? Because unless Alice voluntarily lets them into the apartment to repossess the furniture (which, of course, she is smart enought not to do), they will have to go to court before they can take it. It gets expensive to pay for a lawyer and court costs. It also costs quite a bit to come and take it away—especially when used furniture isn't worth very much anyway. There is just no way Alice is going to lose her furniture, so she should stop worrying about that.

Alice should try informal means to solve her financial problems. Bankruptcy is a drastic remedy, and Alice doesn't want to use it unless she has to. Things may get worse, and if Alice files for bankruptcy now she won't be able to use her bankruptcy protection again when she really needs it. Therefore, Alice should try to negotiate with the finance company. Maybe they will agree to take a smaller amount over a longer period of time. If Alice tells them she is thinking of filing for bankruptcy, maybe they will be a little more cooperative. Because if Alice does file for bankruptcy, she's got an ace in the hole. She gets rid of the debt and gets to keep her household goods too, because this is a special kind of secured debt. The finance company did not loan Alice the money to buy the furniture, so she can keep it— without paying any more for it—after bankruptcy. (See Chapter 5, Step 3.)

*   *   *

EXAMPLE 4: Jake is temporarily unemployed and has barely enough money to feed his old dog Clem, and Annie, his calico cat. He is looking for a job and expects to find one when the economy improves. In the meantime he is being hounded by a collection agency for $4,000 in overdue bills. What should Jake do?

Jake can't file a Chapter 13 plan; he doesn't have a stable and regular source of income. Because he is unemployed, he should not file for bankruptcy—the timing isn't right because he is likely to incur more debts before he gets back on his feet. In addition, since he has no wages and little in the way of savings or other property (and what he has is exempt under state law), he is said to be "judgment proof."

Again, Jake should try informal means to solve his debt problems with an eye to convincing the collection agency not to sue him

26

and get a judgment. It's a little foolish for Jake just to ignore the collection agency because, unlike Lois in Example #1, he expects to be employed soon. Once he does get a job, Jake knows that a portion of his wages will not be an exempt asset, and that a creditor who gets a judgment against him can garnish his wages.

Here are several possible courses of action Jake might consider:

● Offer to pay a very low monthly fee—perhaps interest only—to keep the creditor from suing.

● Offer to pay the collection agency $1,400 in cash now, in full satisfaction of the $4,000 debt. Of course, this depends on Jake having $1,400, but being a resourceful fellow, he can raise it by selling his motorcycle. By offering to pay one-third of the debt, Jake is starting low. He should be prepared for the collection agency to respond by asking for $2,000 or even $2,500 in exchange for cancellation of the debt. But if Jake convinces them $1,400 is all he has, they just might take it.

If his informal efforts are unsuccessful, Jake should think about a Chapter 13 plan or bankruptcy once he gets a job. If his earnings then are large enough, he might try to repay his debts under a Chapter 13 plan. But if his debts have grown, there is no realistic way to pay them off, and wage garnishments are threatened, he probably should file bankruptcy.

* * *

EXAMPLE 5: Paul has a family of five. He is absolutely astounded when he totals his bills—$18,000 and many of them overdue. He is a bus driver and makes $22,000 a year. Paul had no idea he could be that far in debt when nothing special had happened. These were just ordinary living expenses. Paul just shakes his head when he thinks about money—right now the kids need new school clothes. What should Paul do?

It looks like Paul is so deep in debt that straight bankruptcy might be his best solution. But before Paul makes a decision, he should talk to Consumer Credit Counselors. They will help him figure out a monthly budget designed to leave his family enough money to live and to help him to repay his bills over a couple of years. If he doesn't have the income to do it, they will tell him so. By going through a budgetary process, Paul should at least learn something about living within his income.

If Paul does conclude that he can't realistically pay off his obligations, he must take a close look at his debts. If most are nondischargeable in straight bankruptcy, like student loans, Paul should file a Chapter 13 plan and offer to pay whatever he can honestly afford. However, if most are dischargeable in straight bankruptcy, this could well be the way for Paul to go because it seems unlikely that he can repay most of his debts with a Chapter 13 plan.

*   *   *

EXAMPLE 6: Kathy is an airline flight attendant. She used to take home about $1,400 a month. But now her wages have been garnished by a former landlord who has a judgment against her for $3,000. She is unable to meet her ongoing expenses or make any payments on her bills (totalling $7,000) with the $1,050 left in her paycheck after the garnishment. Her mailbox is full of dunning letters and several creditors have instituted lawsuits against her. She is afraid her new sports car will be repossessed. What should Kathy do?

Kathy has to sit down and analyze her debts and property to determine which debts are dischargeable in bankruptcy and Chapter 13 and which property is exempt. She shouldn't panic and let a wage garnishment drive her into legal proceedings until she does this. Like Paul, she has to make a realistic decision about whether it's possible for her to repay her debts.

By the way, Kathy will probably not lose her car by filing straight bankruptcy or a Chapter 13 plan—in fact, these may be two ways for her to keep it. Because her car obligation is a secured debt, in order to retain the car after filing a bankruptcy petition or Chapter 13 plan, Kathy must pay her creditor the present value of the car or the balance due on the loan—whichever is less. The present value will very likely be considerably less than the balance due on the loan, so she will only have to pay that lesser amount.

*   *   *

EXAMPLE 7: Allan graduated from college last year. He borrowed $10,000 in student loans and has made no payments on them. Allan's father co-signed another $3,000 loan to set him up in his apartment and get him outfitted for his new career as a salesman. In addition, Allan has run up about $4,000 in miscellaneous debts. His annual salary is about $17,000 a year. He is being pressured on his student loans and his father is being threatened by the creditor on the note he co-signed. What should Allan do?

Straight bankruptcy will not relieve Allan of his obligation to pay the entire student loan—but Chapter 13 will. If informal negotiations don't work out, Allan might consider filing a Chapter 13 plan. He should be aware, however, that neither straight bankruptcy nor Chapter 13 will protect Allan's father from having to pay the $3,000 loan he co-signed.

* * *

EXAMPLE 8: Sam and Phyllis have about $10,000 of miscellaneous debts. They were doing all right until Phyllis gave up her job when Carole was born. Since then, they can't seem to make ends meet.

Sam and Phyllis bought a three-bedroom house in 1973 for $50,000. Their mortgage is now $32,000. Recently, they had a realtor appraise the home, and she said it is worth about $120,000. What should Sam and Phyllis do?

Like Frank and Paul, Sam and Phyllis should stop by Consumer Credit Counselors and see if they can readjust their expenses to free up some money to repay those debts. If that doesn't work, they still have a couple of good options. If Phyllis doesn't want to return to work yet, they might consider refinancing the house—taking out a second mortgage and using the money to pay off their debts. Of course, that will mean a bigger monthly house payment, but it will be a lot less than the total monthly payments on their outstanding obligations. If Sam and Phyllis can't pay off most of their debts by refinancing the house, they might want to consider filing bankruptcy or a Chapter 13 plan.

CHAPTER

5

$$$$$

UNDERSTANDING YOUR DEBTS

Before you get into the meat of this chapter, pause a moment and learn three important facts about debts.

1. Bankruptcy protects you only against debts in existence as of the date of filing your bankruptcy papers. It will not protect you against new creditors. Timing is important because a bankruptcy discharge is available to you only once every six years.
2. Bankruptcy will not protect anyone but you. If relatives or friends cosigned any of your loans, they will still have to pay them, even though you do not.
3. You should not pay off any debts within three months prior to bankruptcy—your creditors will just have to give back that money to the bankruptcy trustee. If you do want to pay friends or relatives, wait until after you have filed the bankruptcy petition—then they can keep the money.

Now follow the steps below to get a good understanding of your debts and how bankruptcy will affect them.

Step 1. Make a List of Your Debts.   Generally, the filing of a bankruptcy petition will result in a release from debt for the debtor—you will simply not have to pay your creditors any more money. But, as we've discovered, there are some types of debts that are not affected by bankruptcy, so you must continue to pay them. They are called *nondischargeable* debts. If a substantial number of your debts are of this kind, bankruptcy may not be the answer for you.

To find out, first make a list of all your debts on Worksheet 1 in Chapter 6. Do this now. (You may want to tear the worksheet out of the book.) Your list will probably include many of the following items:

rent
house payments
utility bills
car payments
oil company credit card purchases
department store credit card purchases
debts to finance companies
doctor bills
hospital bills
attorneys' fees
court costs
collection agency fees
repossession fees
debts on repossessed goods
alimony and child support
civil suits
bail bonds
student loans
loans from friends or relatives
record, book, or magazine club purchases

Step 2. Decide Which Debts Are Dischargeable. Make a separate column of all those debts on the list that are in fact wiped out in bankruptcy. To do this you will have to carefully read the next pages to understand what kinds of debts are discharged in bankruptcy and what kinds are not.

The most common types of debts that are *not* dischargeable and that follow you past bankruptcy are as follows:

1. *Spousal support (alimony) and child support.* These are not dischargeable. Also, in some situations, if the divorce decree ordered you to pay debts incurred during marriage, you may have a legal obligation to your spouse to do so—even after bankruptcy. It all depends on whether your obligation to pay debts is either a kind of (nondischargeable) hidden support to your spouse or simply a (dischargeable) part of a division of your marital property and debts. This can be a rather technical question, so you should check with an attorney.

2. *Student loans.* Whether they are direct, insured, or guaranteed, student loans are not dischargeable in bankruptcy if they are owed to a governmental body or a nonprofit institution of higher education. There are several exceptions to this rule, however. Student loans are dischargeable if they first became due at least five years ago. Since student loans usually do not become due until nine months after you leave school, you could discharge your student loans by filing bankruptcy March 2, 1982 if you graduated from college June 1, 1976. You can also discharge student loans if making you pay them would "impose an undue hardship" on you and your family. It is not clear yet what circumstances might amount to that kind of hardship, so if you have unpaid student loans that are causing you a serious hardship, check with an attorney about recent legal developments in this area.

3. *State or federal income taxes.* Income taxes are not dischargeable in bankruptcy if they were due within the past three years. Nor are they dischargeable if you filed a fraudulent return, failed to file a return at all, or filed a late return for an earlier year's taxes within the last three years. They are dischargeable if the taxes were due more than three years ago, and if a timely and nonfraudulent return was filed. This means that if you filed an honest return on time every year, you can in May 1984 discharge in bankruptcy taxes on income you earned before or during 1980.

4. *Auto accident claims where driver was drunk or reckless.* If a court so determines, a claim against you resulting from an automobile accident is not dischargeable in bankruptcy. This happens only if you were in serious violation of proper driving rules, like drunk driving, hit and run, or driving on the wrong side of the road. Claims from accidents which involve ordinary negligence are dischargeable. If you are in doubt, see an attorney about this, because the right to discharge here is very dependent on the facts.

5. *Fines.* Traffic tickets and fines for violation of the law in criminal cases are not dischargeable in bankruptcy. (Yes, traffic violations are really criminal offenses of a petty nature.)

6. *Debts incurred using fraudulent statements.* If a court so determines, debts incurred by use of false financial statements are not dischargeable in bankruptcy. For example, if you borrowed money from a finance company, you probably had to fill out and sign a

BANKRUPTCY: DO IT YOURSELF

list of your assets, the names of your creditors and the amount of debt owed to each one, and your monthly income. If you deliberately omitted some of your creditors or exaggerated the amount of your income or assets, you have made a false financial statement. But what if you were misled or encouraged not to list some of your debts—perhaps by the statement of the lender that he or she wanted you to list only some of your debts and was not interested in small bills? If yours was an innocent mistake, or you were tricked into making an error on the financial statement, the debt may still be discharged. Consult an attorney about your particular situation.

7. *Fraud.* If a court so determines, debts for property or money you obtained by fraud are not dischargeable in bankruptcy. For example, if you paid for a new TV with a check that bounced, the debt will not be discharged if you knew that there wasn't enough money in your account to cover the check. (Besides, your criminal record resulting from this kind of trick will also follow you beyond bankruptcy.) Again, see an attorney about this. In addition, if a court so determines, very recent credit purchases or credit card purchases are not dischargeable in bankruptcy if you had already decided on bankruptcy when the purchases were made. The idea here is very simple: don't try to take advantage of the bankruptcy system. It doesn't work. Bankruptcy is not a license to steal. Those debts won't go away. Once you decide to file for bankruptcy, stop incurring any more debts. You may ask how a court would know the precise moment when you decided to file. They won't, but they assume that most debtors don't go on spending sprees, so if you run up a lot of bills just prior to filing for bankruptcy, you can be pretty sure that an effort will be made to deny the discharge of those debts.

8. *Debts you forgot to list.* Debts that you forget to put down on the bankruptcy forms discussed in Chapter 8 are not dischargeable in bankruptcy. You might be surprised to know that thousands of people don't get all their debts wiped out simply because they forget to list them. Play it safe. List everything, including those debts you plan to pay anyway, debts you believe will not be pursued, and debts that someone claims you owe even if you do not believe you owe them. And when you have finished, check your list and then recheck it.

IMPORTANT: Honesty is a good idea! You may be denied a discharge from *all* of your debts (and wind up worse off than before you started) if you try to conceal major objects of your property. As you will see in Chapter 7, you will probably get to keep most of your property anyway, because of state or federal exemption laws. So do not give any major items of property such as cash or a car to friends or relatives, or ask them to keep (hide) property for you. If you try this, you might be charged with a crime. It is also contrary to law to sell property for less than it is worth just prior to bankruptcy. Finally, when you fill out the forms described in Chapter 8, be sure to list all your property at a reasonably honest value, given its age and present condition. This is normally the amount at which you could sell it if you had a garage sale or put an ad in the paper. This doesn't mean that you have to be paranoid. If your car can reasonably be said to be worth somewhere between $800 and $1,200, you can list it at $800; but don't try to claim it's worth only $300.

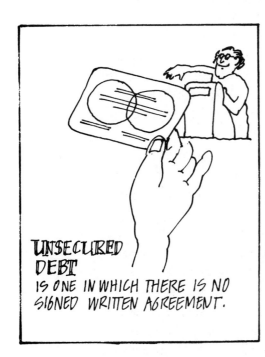

UNSECURED DEBT IS ONE IN WHICH THERE IS NO SIGNED WRITTEN AGREEMENT.

SECURED DEBT IS ONE IN WHICH YOU SIGN A CONTRACT PLEDGING AN ITEM OF YOUR PROPERTY IF YOU FAIL TO PAY.

Step 3. Decide Which of Your Debts Are Secured Debts. Remember when we mentioned in Chapter 3 that in addition to understanding the terms *dischargeable debt* and *nondischargeable debt,* you should also fully understand what *secured* and *unsecured* debts are? Well, here we are—if you haven't already done so, the time to gain that understanding is at hand. Despite what you may imagine, the whole concept is pretty easy, although it can seem confusing at first.

Unsecured Debts Defined

An unsecured debt is created when you buy something or borrow money and do not make a written pledge of some of your property as collateral in the event you fail to pay.

If you bought a new couch and used your bank credit card to pay, you incurred an unsecured debt.

If you bought a new suit at a department store and had the clerk put the bill on your store charge account, you incurred an unsecured debt.

If you borrowed money from your credit union in the form of a "personal" loan or "signature" loan—so that you offered none of your property as security for the repayment of the loan—you incurred an unsecured debt.

Unless they fall into one of the categories discussed in Step 1, unsecured debts are dischargeable in bankruptcy—they disappear. And you are free to keep any property you bought, provided it is exempt property.

Secured Debts Defined

A secured debt is created when you buy something or borrow money and make a written promise saying that if you do not pay, the seller or creditor can repossess some of your property.

If you bought a television set on credit and signed a written agreement saying that your new TV was "security" for the balance owing on its purchase price, either at the time of purchase or earlier when you opened the charge account, you incurred a secured debt.

If you borrowed money from your credit union to buy a stereo and signed a written agreement saying that your new stereo was "collateral" for the loan, you incurred a secured debt.

If you borrowed money to buy your car, and the creditor's name is on the ownership and registration papers, you incurred a secured debt.

Be sure to check and see whether any of your obligations are secured debts. The most likely ones are debts for the purchase of motor vehicles, furniture, appliances, television sets, stereos, and jewelry. If you are in doubt, ask the creditor for a copy of any written agreement you may have signed. You have a right to a copy. If it is called a conditional sales agreement or security agreement, and provides either that the seller will retain title to the goods until the purchase price is paid or that the purchased goods are security for the balance of the purchase price, the obligation is a secured debt. It should not be difficult to determine whether a debt is secured, but if you can't decide, check with an attorney.

What It Means to Have a Secured Debt

As mentioned earlier, secured debts are classified into two categories for the purpose of bankruptcy: "Purchase money secured debts" are the most common. They are created if the secured creditor actually sells you the pledged property or lends you the money to buy it. In order to keep that property after bankruptcy, you must pay the creditor either the balance due on the loan or the present fair market value of the property, whichever is less. If the fair market value is much less than the loan balance due (as well may be the case with second-hand furniture or a rapidly depreciating automobile), bankruptcy will help you to pay only the lesser amount. But if you are unable to pay that amount, you may not keep the item, even though it is of the type classified as exempt property. You must keep your promise to the creditor and give the property back.

"Nonpurchase money secured debts" are created if you pledge property as collateral for a loan and the purpose of the loan has no relation to the property. For example, a debt consolidation loan obtained by pledging your furniture as collateral is a non-purchase money secured loan. If the property you pledged is exempt household goods, that loan will disappear when you file bankruptcy and you can keep the property. You do not have to pay the finance company anything in order to keep these goods. This is a recent change in the law, so if you were told something else in the past, forget it.[1] Unfortunately, though, this exception is not automatic in some bankruptcy courts. You may have to file extra papers with the court in order to keep the secured household property.[2] Check with the bankruptcy clerk to find out the rule in your area.

Again, this material can be a little hard to follow at first. But it's really important that you understand it thoroughly. So reread this section until you are sure you have it and then check your knowledge with the examples that follow.

Lenny bought a new car two years ago for $7,000. He borrowed $5,000 of the money from a bank that is listed as a secured creditor on the ownership certificate. Lenny filed for bankruptcy last week. At that time, the amount of the unpaid balance on the loan was $3,300. The value of the car was $3,000. In order to keep the car, Lenny must pay the bank $3,000, the present value of the car (which is less than the $3,300 unpaid loan balance). If Lenny doesn't want to keep the car, he should tell the bank and they will pick up the car. Lenny's debt for the car will be wiped out in bankruptcy.

*   *   *

Sandra bought a stereo system on the installment plan and signed an agreement that provided that the stereo was security for the payment of the purchase price. The stereo cost $1,800, but if Sandra tried to sell the stereo today, she could get only $1,000 for it. She still owes $500 on the stereo equipment. If Sandra wants to keep the stereo after bankruptcy, she must pay the store $500, the present amount of the debt (which is less than $1,000, the present value of the stereo). If she does not pay off the debt, it will be discharged in bankruptcy, but the store can repossess the stereo.

*　　*　　*

Barbara took out a quick cash loan for $750 from a finance company. She signed a "chattel mortgage" that provided that all of her household goods were security for the repayment of the loan. The debt to the finance company will be wiped out in bankruptcy and Barbara can keep her household goods, free of any claim by the finance company. Why? Because as we learned earlier, only when the security agreement is written by the seller or creditor who loaned the money to buy those very goods (as in the first two examples) must you return the goods or pay for them.

*　　*　　*

Elsie is a single parent. She went out of her way to see that the kids had a nice Christmas last year. She bought them lots of new clothes and toys at a discount store and paid the clerk with a major credit card. Then Elsie's financial affairs took a real turn for the worse and she filed for bankruptcy. The credit card debt will be discharged in bankruptcy. And Elsie won't have to worry about the creditor taking away her daughter's bike or her son's pogo stick. This is an unsecured debt. It will disappear in bankruptcy and Elsie and her kids will be free to keep the items she bought because they are exempt property.

If you're still confused by the mysteries of dischargeable versus nondischargeable and secured versus unsecured debts, the following flowchart might help.

Debt Flow Chart

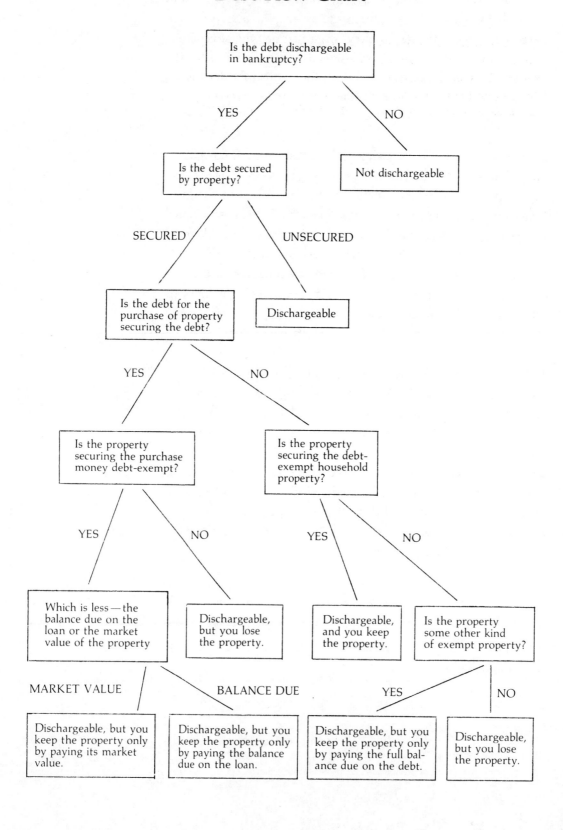

NOTES

1. This law applies only to debts incurred after November 6, 1978. If you created a secured debt prior to that date, you cannot set aside the lien. In order to keep the property, you must pay the creditor either the amount of the debt or the present value of the property, whichever is less.
2. The form of those papers is set out in detail in Chapter 10.

CHAPTER

6

$ $ $ $ $

FILLING OUT YOUR WORKSHEETS; SUMMARIZING YOUR DEBTS

This chapter contains worksheets for you to fill out. We have already referred to several of them earlier in the book. Before you fill out your own worksheets, carefully examine the samples made out in the name of Oscar Lindstrom. Oscar has a lot of the same problems as you, and it will make your job easier to see how he filled out his papers.

NOTE: If you haven't already done so, establish a safe place for all the papers relating to your bankruptcy. Manila file folders or large envelopes work well. Keep your papers neatly organized — bankruptcy is not the time for sloppy work.

OSCAR'S WORKSHEETS

Sample Worksheet 1

Debts of Oscar Lindstrom, a Gardener

Creditor	Amount	Dischargeable?
Truvalo University, for student loans (first due 3/76)	$ 3,000	No—unless an "undue hardship" or five years have passed since they were due. See an attorney.
Anna Lindstrom, for past-due spousal support and child support	$ 700	No.
State Bank, for car loan (secured)—(value of car is $1,500)	$ 1,100	Not really. This is a secured loan. In order to keep the car, Oscar will have to pay the debt, which is less than the present value of the car (see Chapter 10).
Friendly Finance, for vacation loan (secured by household goods), (cosigned by mother)	$ 1,800	Yes—and Oscar can keep the household goods, but his mother will have to pay the debt (see Chapter 5, Step 3).
Bancocard, for miscellaneous purchases	$ 970	Yes.
Otto Lindstrom (Oscar's brother), for personal loan	$ 250	Yes. If Oscar wishes to repay his brother, he should do so *after* bankruptcy.
Wearforever Clothes Store, for clothing	$ 310	Yes.
County of Erehwon, for traffic tickets	$ 110	No.

Fred's Appliance Store, for television set (secured) — (value of TV is $200)		Partially. In order to keep the TV, Oscar will have to pay $200, the present value of the set, but at least he won't have to pay the whole $400 due.
	$ 400	
Driveon Oil Company, for credit card purchases	$ 240	Yes.
Big Man Health Club, for membership	$ 980	Yes.
Dr. Tyler	$ 280	Yes.
Memorial Hospital	$ 925	Yes.
City Utility Company	$ 80	Yes.
Hilda Schwartz, for auto accident (Oscar was uninsured)	$ 1,600	Yes. Oscar checked with an attorney and, like most auto accidents, this one is dischargeable.
Total Debts	$12,745	
Nondischargeable debts (debts Oscar *must* pay after bankruptcy)	$ 3,810	($3,000 + $700 + $110)
Dischargeable secured debts (to keep the car and TV, Oscar must pay)	$ 1,300	($1,100 + $200)
Debts Oscar wants to repay after bankruptcy		
Friendly Finance (his mother cosigned this loan)	$ 1,800	
Otto Lindstrom (his brother)	$ 250	
Debts Oscar is free of after bankruptcy	$ 5,385	($970 + $310 + $240 + $980 + $280 + $925 + $80 + $1,600)

45

Sample Worksheet 2

Oscar Lindstrom's After-Bankruptcy Budget

Take-home pay	$1,225/month
Expenses:	
Rent	$200
Utilities	25
Food	160
Clothing	20
Medical care	20
Entertainment	80
Transportation (gas)	40
Miscellaneous — auto insurance premium	25
Debt — Monthly Payments:	
Spousal and child support (current and overdue)	400
Student loans (current and overdue)	100
Car payment (to secured creditor)	75
TV payment (to secured creditor)	25

To brother (personal loan)	20
To mother (who cosigned his debt to Friendly Finance)	20
Total expenses	$1,210
Income	$1,225
Expenses	1,210
	$ 15 to spare

Sample Worksheet 3

Should Oscar Lindstrom Declare Bankruptcy?

Take-home pay	$ 1,225/month $14,700/year
Dischargeable debts:	
Bancocard	$ 970
Wearforever Clothes	310
Driveon Oil	240
Big Man Health Club	980
Dr. Tyler	280

Memorial Hospital	925
City Utility Company	80
Hilda Schwartz	1,600
	$5,385

Oscar's dischargeable debts are approximately 37 percent of his annual take-home pay. Note that Oscar did not include in his calculations the following obligations, either debts he wants to repay after bankruptcy or secured debts where he wants to keep the property:

Friendly Finance (cosigned by mother and Oscar wants to repay her)	$1,800
Otto Lindstrom (Oscar wants to repay his brother)	250
State Bank (secured by car, which Oscar wants to keep; in order to do so, he must pay $1,100, the amount of the debt)	1,100
Fred's Appliance Store (secured by television, which Oscar wants to keep; in order to do so, he must pay $200, the value of the TV)	400

YOUR WORKSHEETS

You have three worksheets to fill out. Instructions for Worksheet 1 are contained in Chapter 5, Steps 1 and 2. Your second worksheet is your budget after bankruptcy. Be realistic! And remember, if your budget doesn't come out so that you are in the black after bankruptcy, it is not wise to file now. Worksheet 3 will also help you decide whether or not you should file for bankruptcy now. You will want to restudy Chapter 4 as you fill out this one.

Your Worksheet 1

Your Debts
(Refer to Chapter 5, Steps 1 and 2 for instructions.)

Creditor	Amount	Dischargeable?
Student loans		
Taxes		
Alimony or child support		
Rent or mortgage payments		
Utilities		
Home repairs		
Car loans and auto repairs		
Finance companies		
Personal loans		
Charge account purchases		
Credit card purchases		
Medical bills		
Miscellaneous		

Total Debts

Nondischargeable debts
(debts you must pay
after bankruptcy)

Dischargeable secured debts
(debts you must pay
in order to keep property)

Debts you want to repay
after bankruptcy

Debts you are free of
after bankruptcy

Your Worksheet 2

Your Budget After Bankruptcy

Take-home pay

Expenses

Rent

Utilities

Food

Clothing

Entertainment

Transportation

Medical care

Insurance (auto, renter's, homeowner's, health, life)

Miscellaneous

Monthly debt payments

Total Expenses

Total Monthly Income _____

Total Monthly Expenses -_____

_____ **What You Have Left**

Your Worksheet 3

Should You Declare Bankruptcy?

(Refer to Chapter 4)

Take-home Pay

Dischargeable Debts
(Do not include debts
that you plan to pay.)

/Month
/Year

What percentage?

Annual
Take-home) Dischargeable Debts
Pay

CHAPTER

7

$$$$$

UNDERSTANDING YOUR PROPERTY

In theory, the federal bankruptcy law states that a bankrupt must surrender some of his or her property in exchange for the forgiveness of debt. Don't worry—this does not mean that you will lose the covers from your bed, the clothes from your back, the food on your table, or the roof over your head. Indeed, you may not lose any property at all. Why? Because both state and federal laws allow a debtor to keep what is called *exempt property*. The idea is that people who declare bankruptcy should be allowed to retain fundamental items to aid them in their quest for a fresh start. This means that the bankruptcy trustee will take only property that is nonexempt as part of the bankruptcy proceedings. If you have nonexempt property, the trustee will sell it and divide the money among your creditors. If all your property is exempt, the bankruptcy trustee won't take anything.

In order to make an intelligent decision about whether or not bankruptcy is wise for you, you will need to know what property you may keep for yourself (exempt property) and what property you must surrender to the bankruptcy trustee (nonexempt property). Make a list of all your property on the worksheet at the end of this chapter. Do this now. Then, as you read this chapter through, fill in the worksheet with information as to whether the property is or is not exempt.

A person who declares bankruptcy generally has a choice between two separate exemption systems—one state and the other federal.[1] You can choose either one, but you can't choose some of one and some of the other. This will become clear as we go along. It is up to you to compare your state exemption system with the federal exemption system and decide which will be the most advantageous in your situation.

REMEMBER: It is perfectly all right to convert some of your nonexempt property to exempt property before you file for bankruptcy. Just don't give any of your property away or sell it for less than it's worth—this may cause you to lose that all-important discharge from debt. If you are in doubt about this, reread the first five chapters of this book.

YOUR STATE EXEMPTION SYSTEM

The exemption systems for all states are listed in Appendix A. Turn to your state exemption system now and read it. Many of these statutes have not been revised since the turn of the century. If you think it looks like they were meant for a rural America, you're right. They were.

Perhaps in your state there is a distinction made between types of debtors—a "head of family" or "householders" and others. Although the definitions vary from state to state, a "head of family" or "householder" is usually defined as either a married person or a person who has members of the family living with him or her in the same household. If your state makes this distinction and you are not sure if you qualify for this special category of debtors, check with an attorney.

The exemption system of each state has been divided into a number of categories:

1. *Homestead.* Some states exempt the family residence. In order to claim this exemption, it is necessary in most such states to file a formal Declaration of Homestead prior to bankruptcy. Therefore, if you own real property, you should check with an attorney about this.

    In most states, the homestead exemption is limited to a certain value. Let's look at a couple of examples to see how the limitations in value are applied.

    Charlie and his wife Joan bought a little one-bedroom house in California in 1976 for $40,000. They paid $8,000 down and now owe $29,000 on their only mortgage. Similar houses in the neighborhood are now selling at $60,000. If Charlie and Joan file for bankruptcy, they will be able to keep their home because their equity is less than $45,000, the exempt value allowed a head of household by California statute.

    $60,000 market value
    - 29,000 mortgage (present amount)
    _____
    $31,000 total equity

    *   *   *

    Elaine and her roommate together bought their New York apartment when it was converted to a condominium in 1978. They paid $6,000 down on a purchase price of $60,000 and now owe $51,000 on the mortgage. Other condominiums in the same building are now selling for $70,000. Elaine and her roommate own the condominium jointly, so that each has a one-half interest in the equity.

$70,000 market value
- 51,000 mortgage (present amount)
_____
$19,000 total equity

Elaine's 50 percent interest in the equity is $9,500. If Elaine files for bankruptcy, she will be able to keep her financial interest in the condominium because that interest is less than $10,000, the exempt value allowed by New York statute.

* * *

Sam and Phyllis bought a three-bedroom house in Massachusetts in 1973 for $50,000. They recently had a realtor appraise the home, and were told that it is now worth about $120,000. If Sam and Phyllis file for bankruptcy, they will lose their home because their equity is greater than the $50,000 maximum equity exempt under Massachusetts law.

$120,000 market value
− 32,000 mortgage (present amount)
_____
$ 88,000 total equity (of which only $50,000 is
       exempt)

Because their equity is greater than the exempt value allowed by statute, if Sam and Phyllis file for bankruptcy, the trustee will sell the home and give them $50,000 from the sale proceeds. The other $38,000 will be used to pay for the costs of sale and then to pay off their creditors. If their debts are less than $38,000, Sam and Phyllis will get the rest of the sales proceeds back, less the costs of sale.

There is a way for Sam and Phyllis to keep their house and perhaps avoid bankruptcy altogether. They can refinance the house — take out a second mortgage and use the money to pay off their debts. Of course that will mean a bigger monthly house payment, but it will be a lot less than the total monthly payments on their outstanding obligations.

UNDERSTANDING YOUR PROPERTY

If you won't be able to pay off most of your debts by refinancing your house, you may want to consider bankruptcy. In that event, you should borrow at least enough against your house to reduce the equity to within the exempt value allowed by your state statute and thereby keep your house. Then use the loan proceeds to acquire other exempt property.

2. *Wages.* Federal law (15 United States Code 1673) allows a debtor to exempt three-fourths of the wages not yet paid for the work the debtor has done in the past thirty days. If your state has a more generous exemption, you may claim it. If your state does not have a more generous exemption, you may exempt three-fourths of your wages by claiming the federal wage exemption.

   You can often keep all of your wages by filing for bankruptcy the day after payday, after cashing your paycheck, and using the money to buy some other exempt asset. If your work period does not correspond with your pay period so that you will still be owed wages on payday (perhaps you are paid each week for work done two weeks earlier), you should ask for an advance from your employer to cover your wages in the week immediately preceding your bankruptcy filing. Otherwise, you risk losing a percentage of your earned but unpaid wages in bankruptcy. If you have vacation pay coming, you should ask for an advance on this also.

3. *Tools of trade.* These are the things you use to earn a living. For example, a gardener might classify as exempt property his or her truck, lawnmower, rake, shovel, hoe, and clippers. If you have work tools but are not presently employed, or are not using these items in your present job, or use these items only in a second job, or plan to claim a motor vehicle as a tool of trade, consult an attorney.

4. *Personal property.* Most states exempt food, necessary household furnishings, and wearing apparel. In many states there is no dollar limit on this exemption, simply the subjective notion of what is "necessary." The idea of necessity depends on your lifestyle prior to bankruptcy. In some states people have been able to keep sterling silver, crystal, and even mink coats because they had lived rather nicely prior to bankruptcy. How *you* lived prior to bankruptcy is the key. Don't try to trade nonexempt property for lavish items right before bankruptcy. It doesn't work, unless that's

the way you're used to living. And if you do have any unusual and expensive household items — like oriental rugs or antique furniture — it might be wise to consult an attorney.

Some states exempt your equity in a motor vehicle within certain dollar limits. Compute the equity in the same manner you computed your equity in your home. Market value is determined by reference to the Blue Book; select the lowest value listed for your car. If your car is too old to be listed in the Blue Book, determine its value by looking at classified ads in the newspapers. Again, let's look at a couple of examples:

Ted owns an old beat-up 1963 Volkswagen, free and clear. When ads for similar cars appear in the newspaper, the asking price is about $400. If Ted files for bankruptcy in California, he can keep his car, because it is worth less than $1200.

Luke has a big, expensive motorcycle. He bought it for $2,800. It is now worth about $2,000 — and Luke still owes $1,600 on it. Luke's $400 equity ($2,000 value minus $1,600 still owed) is exempt, but Luke has another problem. The motorcycle is collateral for a secured debt. If Luke files for bankruptcy in California, he can keep his motorcycle — but only if he pays the secured creditor $1,600. (See Chapter 5, Step 3 if you don't understand this.)

5. *Insurance.* In many states, a life insurance policy is exempt, but only if the beneficiary is someone other than the debtor. Carefully check your beneficiary designation with your insurance agent prior to bankruptcy.

6. *Pensions.* Veterans' benefits (45 USC 352(E)), Social Security benefits (42 USC 407), civil service retirement benefits (5 USC 729 and 2265), Railroad Retirement Act annuities and pensions (45 USC 228(L)), Foreign Service Retirement and Disability payments (22 USC 1104), and Longshoremen's and Harbor Workers' Compensation Act death and disability benefits (33 USC 916), are exempt under federal law.

7. *Public benefits.* Almost all states exempt public assistance, worker's compensation, and unemployment insurance.

Now we're halfway through. You should have marked your worksheet to show which of your items of property are exempt under state law. Sit back and relax a minute before you go on.

Okay, now examine your worksheet. You may find that most of your property is exempt from being taken when you file for bankruptcy. If so, great. If not, and you find that you have a lot of nonexempt assets—things like expensive sporting goods or cameras, stamp and coin collections, musical instruments, power tools, a typewriter—don't panic! The fact that assets are not exempt doesn't necessarily mean you're going to lose them. Although technically the trustee has a right to take all nonexempt property, he or she will normally decide not to bother with items that have very little market value (under $50) or items that will cost too much to collect, care for, and sell (for example, a middle-aged pedigreed dog). There. That saved some of your property, didn't it? But there still may be a couple of items in jeopardy. Remember that you can always sell them and convert the money into exempt property. For example, a new electric typewriter could be turned into $500 that could be used to buy food. But if you don't want to sell your property, or for some reason can't easily sell these nonexempt items and convert them into exempt assets, you may wish to elect the federal exemption system.

REMINDER: You must choose either the state or the federal exemption system. You can't mix the two. In some states, the federal exemption system is not available. Double check the availability of the federal exemptions in your state in Appendix A before reading on.

THE FEDERAL EXEMPTION SYSTEM

Under the federal exemption system, a person may keep the following:

1. A residence of any kind—a house, condominium, house trailer, mobile home, houseboat, or boat—and a burial plot, with a total equity of $7,500, computed the same way as in the state homestead exemption (11 USC 522 (d) (1)).
2. A motor vehicle with an equity of $1,200, computed the same way as in the state personal property exemption (11 USC 522 (d) (2)).
3. An equity of $200 *per item* of household furnishings, household goods, wearing apparel, appliances, books, animals, crops, and musical instruments (11 USC 522 (d) (3)). Remember that the value of an item is its present fair market value if you had to sell it at a garage sale or through the want ads, not what you paid for it.

4. $500 total equity of all jewelry (11 USC 522 (d) (4)).

5. $750 total equity of all implements, professional books, or tools of trade (11 USC 522 (d) (6)).

6. $4,000 cash value of life insurance (11 USC 522 (d) (8)).

7. Health insurance benefits (11 USC 522 (d) (10)).

8. Disability benefits (11 USC 522 (d) (10)).

9. Retirement benefits including stock bonus, pension, profit sharing, and annuity plans (11 USC 522 (d) (10)).

10. Unemployment compensation (11 USC 522 (d) (10)).

11. Public assistance (11 USC 522 (d) (10)).

12. Veterans' benefits (11 USC 522 (d) (10)).

13. Social Security benefits (11 USC 522 (d) (10)).

14. Awards under a crime victim's reparation law (11 USC 522 (d) (11)).

15. $7,500 of payments on account of a personal bodily injury (not including payments for pain and suffering or lost earnings) and 100 percent of payments in compensation for loss of future earnings (11 USC 522 (d) (11)).

16. $400 in any property *plus* any unused amount of exemption 1 (11 USC 522 (d) (5)). This is important. In addition to the property designated in exemptions 2-15, if you do not own a residence, you may claim as exempt property $7,900 of anything else. This last exemption may enable you to keep otherwise nonexempt items — like tax refunds, bank accounts, savings bonds or stocks and bonds, your boat, or your stamp collection. Or it may protect your entire equity in an expensive exempt asset such as your car, jewelry, stereo, piano, or rare trained ostrich.

It is the last exemption alone that will cause many debtors to elect the federal over the state system, unless they own equities of over $7,500 in their dwellings, and those equities are protected by their respective state homestead statutes. It is generous in amount and avoids much of the hassle under the state system of converting nonexempt property to exempt form. Nonetheless, make sure you compute your exempt property under both your state and the federal system. Then decide which is better for you.[2] Again, remember that you must select one system or the other. You cannot pick and choose the best exemptions from each system. And unless you elect the federal system, you cannot substitute nonexempt property for an unused exemption.

WHICH EXEMPTION SYSTEM SHOULD YOU CHOOSE?

Rather than just repeating the preceding points, let's look at a couple of examples.

Shirley owns a car worth $1750, a harp worth $3500, and a nine-year-old purebred cocker spaniel named Janice. She also has a checking account with a present balance of $150 and a savings account at a bank with a present balance of $200.

Under California law, none of her property is exempt. Unless Shirley sells all her property before she files for bankruptcy and closes her bank accounts and puts the money in some exempt asset, she will lose all of it—except her dog, which (with all due respect to Janice) isn't worth enough for the trustee to bother with. When the trustee does take her car, however, Shirley will get in exchange $1200 in cash, the amount of the state exemption for motor vehicles. But if Shirley picks the federal exemption system, she can keep all her property without bothering about specific exemptions or property transfers because it is worth less than $7900.

Herb and Greta own a home in Massachusetts. The present amount of the mortgage is $75,000 and the present value of the home, based on recent sales in the neighborhood, is $105,000. The difference is the "equity" of $30,000. In addition to furniture and furnishings, they own a $1,000 car free and clear and have some expensive fishing gear that might be worth $200 at a garage sale.

Like most homeowners, Herb and Greta should pick their state's exemption system because it will protect up to $50,000 of equity in their home. The federal exemption system would protect only $15,000 (two times $7,500 because they are two people). They must either sell the car or borrow against it and put the money in a bank (an exempt asset), because Massachusetts law allows them to keep a vehicle worth only $700. They should also sell the fishing gear and use the sale proceeds to buy food (an exempt asset).

What happens if Herb and Greta just "forget" to list the fishing gear on their forms? They will be taking a serious chance. If the trustee ever finds out that they weren't entirely truthful, they may lose their discharge from debt and be charged with a crime as well.

TIMING PROBLEMS IN FILING BANKRUPTCY

In general, everything you acquire after the date you file for bankruptcy is yours to keep—whether it is exempt or not. There are, however, several exceptions you should be aware of:

1. Tax refunds due (but not received) when bankruptcy is filed (whether you have filed your return yet or not). Do not cash the checks when they arrive after the bankruptcy, as they must be surrendered to the trustee—unless you can claim them as an exempt asset under federal exemption 16. If you can't and they are big enough, you might consider delaying bankruptcy until you receive them and have a chance to convert them into the form of an exempt asset.

2. An inheritance or the proceeds of a life insurance policy, if the individual leaving the money or policy dies within six months after the date of the bankruptcy filing. This means that if in the near future you expect to take something by someone's death, you should consult your attorney about your situation.

3. Payments made by an insurance company for losses suffered prior to the bankruptcy filing but not yet received at the time of the bankruptcy. You may wish to collect any claims for lost, stolen, or damaged property before you file, unless you can claim them as an exempt asset under federal exemption 16.

4. Money you recover in a lawsuit, even if received after your bankruptcy, if you had a right to file the lawsuit prior to the bankruptcy filing. Check with an attorney before you file if you believe you have a legal claim against someone.

Sample Worksheet 4

Property of Oscar Lindstrom, a gardener

Asset	Value	Exempt? California	Federal
1978 Chevrolet Caprice (secured debt of $1,100)	$2,000	Yes—equity of $900.*	Yes.*
American Bank Christmas Club Account Checking Account Savings Account	120 350 475	No. Oscar should close these accounts and use the money to buy exempt assets.	No—but Oscar may count them toward the $7,900 exemption.
U.S. Savings Bonds	250	No. Oscar should cash the savings bonds and use the money to buy exempt assets.	No—but Oscar may count them toward the $7,900 exemption.
Life Insurance Policy with Prudent Equity Co.; annual premiums $300, cash value $700, face amount $10,000	700	Yes.	Yes.
Power tools not used in Oscar's business	150	No. Oscar may wish to sell them.	No—but Oscar may count them toward the $7,900 exemption.
Golf clubs	50	No. But the trustee will probably not bother with them.	No—but Oscar may count them toward the $7,900 exemption.
Coin collection	175	No. Oscar may wish to sell it.	No—but Oscar may count them toward the $7,900 exemption.
Wearing apparel	100	Yes.	Yes.

Asset	Value	Exempt?	
		California	Federal
Stereo	300	Yes.	No—it is worth more than $200; Oscar may count $100 of the value toward the $7,900 exemption.
Couch	100	Yes.	Yes.
Bed	75	Yes.	Yes.
Chest	20	Yes.	Yes.
Breakfast set	60	Yes.	Yes.
Kitchen goods	45	Yes.	Yes.
Television set (secured debt of $400)	200	Yes.**	Yes.**
Mower, rake, hoe, shovel, clippers	180	Yes—tools of the trade.	Yes—tools of the trade.
Loan to Jane Cleatkens	100	No. Oscar should collect the debt and buy food or some other exempt asset.	No—but Oscar may count this toward the $7,900 exemption.
Tax refund	25	No. Oscar can keep it only if he receives the refund prior to bankruptcy and converts it into an exempt asset.	No—but Oscar may count this toward the $7,900 exemption.

NOTE: If Oscar claims the federal exemption he is able to keep all of his property. If Oscar claims the California exemption, he will have to convert nonexempt assets into exempt assets prior to bankruptcy.

*But, in either case, in order to keep the car, Oscar must pay the creditor the amount of the debt ($1,100) because this is a secured debt. If you don't fully understand the difference between secured and unsecured debts, reread Chapter 5.

**But, in either case, in order to keep the television set, Oscar must pay the creditor the present value of the TV, $200, because this is a secured debt. (Since Oscar discharges the $400 debt by paying $200, he already comes out $200 ahead.)

Your Worksheet 4

Your Property—Is It Exempt?

Asset	Value	Exempt?	
		State	Federal
1. Real property			
2. Car			
3. Bank accounts			
4. Savings bonds			
5. Stock			
6. Tax refunds			
7. Insurance			
8. Furniture			
9. Appliances			
10. Wearing apparel			
11. Jewelry			
12. Sporting goods			
13. Tools			
14. Miscellaneous			

NOTES

1. In Alabama, Alaska, Arizona, Arkansas, Colorado, Delaware, Florida, Georgia, Idaho, Illinois, Indiana, Iowa, Kansas, Kentucky, Louisiana, Maine, Maryland, Missouri, Montana, Nebraska, Nevada, New Hampshire, New York, North Carolina, North Dakota, Ohio, Oklahoma, Oregon, South Carolina, South Dakota, Tennessee, Utah, Virginia, West Virginia and Wyoming, debtors do not have a choice — they must choose the state exemption system.

2. Husband and wife don't have to choose the same exemption system. One can choose state and the other federal. If you think this might be advantageous to you, double check with a lawyer as it can get pretty complicated, particularly in community property states (Louisiana, Texas, New Mexico, California, Nevada, Washington, and Idaho).

HOW TO USE THE FORMS

In the back of this book you will find one complete set of bankruptcy forms. Here are detailed instructions on how to complete each of the forms and where and how to file them. You can tear the forms right out of the book and use them. Relax — you have already done most of the work by preparing your worksheets of debts and property. All you have to do now is transfer the information from your worksheets to the forms. But don't begin to fill in any of the forms until you have read this entire chapter over once. Then tear out the forms, photocopy or cut your worksheets out of the book, and get going. The whole process should only take an evening or so.

A FEW GENERAL INSTRUCTIONS

Use a typewriter to complete each form neatly exactly as shown. If you can't type, photocopy the forms and fill in a set by hand. Then have a friend type the information on the forms you tore out of the book.

Many of the instructions are right on the sample forms. Where longer explanations are needed, you will be directed to detailed instructions that will follow the form.

Don't worry if you run out of room on any of the forms. Just take a blank sheet of white paper, the same size as the forms, label it "Additional Page to (title of form)," and type in the additional data. See Form 4, page 95, for an example.

FILLING IN THE FORMS

Now let's begin filling out each form. Remember, when it gets a little complicated, you will be directed to turn to the special instructions. You can also look at Oscar's sample forms to see how his have been completed. When you are sure you understand all the instructions, take the information from your worksheets and type it on the forms you have torn out of the book.

Filling in these forms is not difficult. You already have all the information you need. But it can be a little tedious, so take your time. You don't have to get all the work done in one sitting.

INSTRUCTIONS FOR FORM 1

Instruction 1: Where Do You File (Which District)? Appendix B is a list of all the bankruptcy courts in the United States. Look in the phone book for the one in your state nearest you. It will be listed under United States Bankruptcy Court. Call the bankruptcy clerk and ask if that is the bankruptcy court for your county, and, if so, the name of the district. You must file in the district where you have resided for at least the last ninety-one days. If you have recently moved, either wait until three months have passed and then file in the district of your current residence, or file right away in the district where you previously resided.

Instruction 2: Your Name Type in the form of your proper name that you most commonly use — for example, either Oscar Lindstrom, or Oscar W. Lindstrom, or O. W. Lindstrom. If you are known by other than your true name or initials, list that other name as well — for example, Oscar Lindstrom, a.k.a. Red Lindstrom. On the next line, type in your Social Security number.

OSCAR LINDSTROM, a.k.a. RED LINDSTROM
S.S. No. 123-45-6789

If you are married, you and your spouse can both file on the same set of forms (and pay only one filing fee instead of two). Just add your spouse's name and Social Security number to the caption.

OSCAR LINDSTROM, a.k.a. RED LINDSTROM
S.S. 123-45-6789

and

INGRID LINDSTROM, a.k.a. INGRID OLSON   (wife's maiden
name)

S.S. No. 321-54-9876

FORM 1

UNITED STATES BANKRUPTCY COURT FOR THE   *See Instruction 1.*   DISTRICT OF

(Type in the name of your state.)   Case No. ◄

*In re

See Instruction 2.

CHAPTER 7   (Leave blank; the clerk will fill this in.)

Debtor   Include here all names used by debtor within last 6 years.

VOLUNTARY CASE: DEBTOR'S *JOINT* PETITION[1]

(If this form is used for joint petitioners wherever the word "petitioner" or words referring to petitioners are used they shall be read as if in the plural.)

1. Petitioner's post-office address is   *(Type in your street address, city, and zip code.)*

2. Petitioner has → ☐ resided within this district for the preceding 180 days.

Mark this box unless you have recently moved; if you have, then mark the last box, and see Instruction 1.

☐ had his *(her)* domicile within this district for the preceding 180 days.

☐ had his *(her)* principal place of business within this district for the preceding 180 days.

☐ resided or been domiciled or had his *(her)* principal place of business within this district for a longer portion of the preceding 180 days than in any other district.

3. Petitioner is qualified to file this petition and is entitled to the benefits of title 11, United States Code as a voluntary debtor.

Wherefore, petitioner prays for relief in accordance with chapter 7 of title 11, United States Code.

Petitioner(s) signs if not represented by attorney

Signed: ....
    Attorney for Petitioner

(You sign here.)

Address: ....
    Petitioner

....
    Petitioner

Type in either your name, or if you are married, your and your spouse's names here.

DECLARATION[2]

INDIVIDUAL: I,   the petitioner named in the foregoing petition, certify under penalty of perjury that the foregoing is true and correct.

JOINT INDIVIDUALS: We,   and   the petitioners named in the foregoing petition, certify under penalty of perjury that the foregoing is true and correct.

CORPORATION: I,   the   of the corporation named as petitioner in the foregoing petition, certify under penalty of perjury that the foregoing is true and correct, and that the filing of this petition on behalf of the corporation has been authorized.

PARTNERSHIP: I,   *a member — an authorized agent —* of the partnership named as petitioner in the foregoing petition, certify under penalty of perjury that the foregoing is true and correct, and that the filing of this petition on behalf of the partnership has been authorized.

Executed on   *(Type in date.)*   19   Signature: ....
    (You sign here.)
    Petitioner

Form Nos. 1 & 2 combined & 5, chapter 7, Voluntary case: debtor's petition individual, joint, corporation and partnership, 10-79.

....
    Petitioner

74

© 1979 JULIUS BLUMBERG, INC.

FORM 1, EXAMPLE

UNITED STATES BANKRUPTCY COURT FOR THE Northern DISTRICT OF California *Case No.*

*In re

OSCAR LINDSTROM
aka RED LINDSTROM
S.S. No. 123-45-6789

Debtor   Include here all names used by debtor within last 6 years.

CHAPTER 7

VOLUNTARY CASE:
DEBTOR'S *JOINT* PETITION[1]

(If this form is used for joint petitioners wherever the word "petitioner" or words referring to petitioners are used they shall be read as if in the plural.)

1. Petitioner's post-office address is   538 Mission Street
San Francisco   CA   94104

2. Petitioner has   ☒ resided within this district for the preceding 180 days.
☐ had his*(her)* domicile within this district for the preceding 180 days.
☐ had his*(her)* principal place of business within this district for the preceding 180 days.
☐ resided or been domiciled or had his*(her)* principal place of business within this district for a longer portion of the preceding 180 days than in any other district.

3. Petitioner is qualified to file this petition and is entitled to the benefits of title 11, United States Code as a voluntary debtor.

Wherefore, petitioner prays for relief in accordance with chapter 7 of title 11, United States Code.

Signed:..
Attorney for Petitioner

Address:...

....

Petitioner(s) signs if not represented by attorney

................*Oscar Lindstrom*................
Petitioner

....
Petitioner

DECLARATION[2]

INDIVIDUAL: I,   OSCAR LINDSTROM   the petitioner named in the foregoing petition, certify under penalty of perjury that the foregoing is true and correct.

JOINT INDIVIDUALS: We,   and   the
petitioners named in the foregoing petition, certify under penalty of perjury that the foregoing is true and correct.

CORPORATION: I,   the   of the corporation named as
petitioner in the foregoing petition, certify under penalty of perjury that the foregoing is true and correct, and that the filing of this petition on behalf of the corporation has been authorized.

PARTNERSHIP: I,   *a member — an authorized agent —* of the partnership named
as petitioner in the foregoing petition, certify under penalty of perjury that the foregoing is true and correct, and that the filing of this petition on behalf of the partnership has been authorized.

Executed on   December 12   19 79   Signature: ......*Oscar Lindstrom*......
Petitioner

....
Petitioner

FORM 2, PAGE 1

UNITED STATES BANKRUPTCY COURT FOR THE *See instruction 1,* **DISTRICT OF** *Type in the name of your* **Case No.**

In re   *See instruction 2, Form 1.*   Form 1.   *state.*

Debtor   Include here all names used by debtor within last 6 years.

STATEMENT OF FINANCIAL AFFAIRS FOR DEBTOR NOT ENGAGED IN BUSINESS

Each question should be answered or the failure to answer explained. If the answer is "none," this should be stated. If additional space is needed for the answer to any question, a separate sheet, properly identified, and made a part hereof, should be used and attached.

The term "original petition," as used in the following questions, shall mean the petition filed under Rule 1002, 1003, or 1004.

(If this form is used by joint debtors wherever the word "debtor" or words referring to debtor are used they shall be read as if in the plural.)

1. Name and residence.
a. What is your full name and social security number?
b. Have you used, or been known by, any other names within the 6 years immediately preceding the filing of the original petition herein? (If so, give particulars.)
c. Where do you now reside?
d. Where else have you resided during the 6 years immediately preceding the filing of the original petition herein?

2. Occupation and income.
a. What is your occupation?
b. Where are you now employed? (Give the name and address of your employer, or the address at which you carry on your trade or profession, and the length of time you have been so employed or engaged.)
c. Have you been in a partnership with anyone, or engaged in any business during the 6 years immediately preceding the filing of the original petition herein? (If so, give particulars, including names, dates, and places.)
d. What amount of income have you received from your trade or profession during each of the 2 calendar years immediately preceding the filing of the original petition herein?
e. What amount of income have you received from other sources during each of these 2 years? (Give particulars, including each source, and the amount received therefrom.)

3. Tax returns and refunds.
a. Where did you file your federal and state income tax returns for the 2 years immediately preceding the filing of the original petition herein?
b. What tax refunds (income and other) have you received during the year immediately preceding the filing of the original petition herein?
c. To what tax refunds (income or other), if any, are you, or may you be, entitled? (Give particulars, including information as to any refund payable jointly to you and your spouse or any other person.)

4. Bank accounts and safe deposit boxes.
a. What bank accounts have you maintained alone or together with any other person, and in your own or any other name within the 2 years immediately preceding the filing of the original petition herein? (Give the name and address of each bank, the name in which the deposit is maintained, and the name and address of every other person authorized to make withdrawals from such account.)
b. What safe deposit box or boxes or other depository or depositories have you kept or used for your securities, cash, or other valuables within the 2 years immediately preceding the filing of the original petition herein? (Give the name and address of the bank or other depository, the name in which each box or other depository was kept, the name and address of every other person who had the right of access thereto, a brief description of the contents thereof, and, if the box has been surrendered, state when surrendered, or, if transferred, when transferred, and the name and address of the transferee.)

5. Books and records.
a. Have you kept books of account or records relating to your affairs within the 2 years immediately preceding the filing of the original petition herein?
b. In whose possession are these books or records? (Give names and addresses.)
c. If any of these books or records are not available, explain.
d. Have any books of account or records relating to your affairs been destroyed, lost or otherwise disposed of within the 2 years immediately preceding the filing of the original petition herein? (If so, give particulars, including date of destruction, loss, or disposition, and reason therefor.)

6. Property held for another person.
What property do you hold for any other person? (Give name and address of each person, and describe the property, or value thereof, and all writings relating thereto.)

7. Prior bankruptcy.
What proceedings under the Bankruptcy Act or title 11, United States Code have previously been brought by or against you? (State the location of the bankruptcy court, the nature and number of each case, the date when it was filed, and whether a discharge was granted or refused, the case was dismissed, or a composition, arrangement, or plan was confirmed.)

1b. *See instructions for Form 2.*

1c. *Type in the street address, city, and county.*

2a. *If you are not working, type in "Unemployed."*

2d. *See instructions for Form 2.*

2e. *See instructions for Form 2.*

3b. *Get this information from your tax returns.*

3c. *See instructions for Form 2.*

4a. *See instructions for Form 2.*

5a. *This includes checkbooks, if you have them.*

6. *If you are keeping property for someone else, list it here. Be prepared to prove it does not belong to you.*

FORM 2, EXAMPLE, PAGE 1

UNITED STATES BANKRUPTCY COURT FOR THE <u>NORTHERN</u>   **DISTRICT OF** CALIFORNIA   *Case No.*

In re   OSCAR LINDSTROM

   aka RED LINDSTROM

Debtor   Include here all names used by debtor within last 6 years.

STATEMENT OF
FINANCIAL AFFAIRS FOR DEBTOR
NOT ENGAGED IN BUSINESS

Each question should be answered or the failure to answer explained. If the answer is "none," this should be stated. If additional space is needed for the answer to any question, a separate sheet, properly identified, and made a part hereof, should be used and attached.

The term "original petition," as used in the following questions, shall mean the petition filed under Rule 1002, 1003, or 1004.

(If this form is used by joint debtors wherever the word "debtor" or words referring to debtor are used they shall be read as if in the plural.)

1. Name and residence.
  a. What is your full name and social security number?
  b. Have you used, or been known by, any other names within the 6 years immediately preceding the filing of the original petition herein?
(If so, give particulars.)
  c. Where do you now reside?
  d. Where else have you resided during the 6 years immediately preceding the filing of the original petition herein?

1a.	OSCAR LINDSTROM, SS No. 123-45-6789
1b.	Yes, Red Lindstrom
1c.	538 Mission St., San Francisco CA 94104
1d.	789 Ocean View, San Francisco CA

2. Occupation and income.
  a. What is your occupation?
  b. Where are you now employed?
(Give the name and address of your employer, or the address at which you carry on your trade or profession, and the length of time you have been so employed or engaged.)
  c. Have you been in a partnership with anyone, or engaged in any business during the 6 years immediately preceding the filing of the original petition herein?
(If so, give particulars, including names, dates, and places.)
  d. What amount of income have you received from your trade or profession during each of the 2 calendar years immediately preceding the filing of the original petition herein?
  e. What amount of income have you received from other sources during each of these 2 years?
(Give particulars, including each source, and the amount received therefrom.)

2a.	Gardener
2b.	Acme Garden Company
	238 Fulton, San Francisco, California
2c.	No
2d.	1977: $12,192 1978: $9,363
2e.	1978: $750 unemployment insurance

3. Tax returns and refunds.
  a. Where did you file your federal and state income tax returns for the 2 years immediately preceding the filing of the original petition herein?
  b. What tax refunds (income and other) have you received during the year immediately preceding the filing of the original petition herein?
  c. To what tax refunds (income or other), if any, are you, or may you be, entitled?
(Give particulars, including information as to any refund payable jointly to you and your spouse or any other person.)

3a.	Federal: Fresno, California
	State: Sacramento, California
3b.	$24.37
3c.	None

4. Bank accounts and safe deposit boxes.
  a. What bank accounts have you maintained alone or together with any other person, and in your own or any other name within the 2 years immediately preceding the filing of the original petition herein?
(Give the name and address of each bank, the name in which the deposit is maintained, and the name and address of every other person authorized to make withdrawals from such account.)
  b. What safe deposit box or boxes or other depository or depositories have you kept or used for your securities, cash, or other valuables within the 2 years immediately preceding the filing of the original petition herein?
(Give the name and address of the bank or other depository, the name in which each box or other depository was kept, the name and address of every other person who had the right of access thereto, a brief description of the contents thereof, and, if the box has been surrendered, state when surrendered, or, if transferred, when transferred, and the name and address of the transferee.)

4a.	American Bank, 33 Main St.
	San Francisco, California: Christmas
	Club account number 35821, checking
	account number 6129758, savings account
	number 531-0798
4b.	None

5. Books and records.
  a. Have you kept books of account or records relating to your affairs within the 2 years immediately preceding the filing of the original petition herein?
  b. In whose possession are these books or records?
(Give names and addresses.)
  c. If any of these books or records are not available, explain.
  d. Have any books of account or records relating to your affairs been destroyed, lost or otherwise disposed of within the 2 years immediately preceding the filing of the original petition herein?
(If so, give particulars, including date of destruction, loss, or disposition, and reason therefor.)

5a.	Yes--checkbook in my possession
5d.	No

6. Property held for another person.
  What property do you hold for any other person?
(Give name and address of each person, and describe the property, or value thereof, and all writings relating thereto.)

6.	None

7. Prior bankruptcy.
  What proceedings under the Bankruptcy Act or title 11, United States Code have previously been brought by or against you?
(State the location of the bankruptcy court, the nature and number of each case, the date when it was filed, and whether a discharge was granted or refused, the case was dismissed, or a composition, arrangement, or plan was confirmed.)

7.	None

FORM 2, PAGE 2

8. Receiverships, general assignments, and other modes of liquidation.

a. Was any of your property, at the time of the filing of the original petition herein, in the hands of a receiver, trustee, or other liquidating agent? (If so, give a brief description of the property, the name and address of the receiver, trustee, or other agent, and, if the agent was appointed in a court proceeding, the name and location of the court the title and number of the case, and the nature of the proceeding.)

b. Have you made any assignment of your property for the benefit of your creditors, or any general settlement with your creditors, within one year immediately preceding the filing of the original petition herein?
(If so, give dates, the name and address of the assignee, and a brief statement of the terms of assignment or settlement.)

9. Property in hands of third person.

Is any other person holding anything of value in which you have an interest? (Give name and address, location and description of the property, and circumstances of the holding.)

10. Suits, executions, and attachments.

a. Were you a party to any suit pending at the time of the filing of the original petition herein? (If so, give the name and location of the court and the title and nature of the proceeding.)

b. Were you a party to any suit terminated within the year immediately preceding the filing of the original petition herein.? (If so, give the name and location of the court, the title and nature of the proceeding, and the result.)

c. Has any of your property been attached, garnished, or seized under any legal or equitable process within the year immediately preceding the filing of the original petition herein? (If so, describe the property seized or person garnished, and at whose suit.)

11. Loans repaid.

What repayments on loans in whole or in part have you made during the year immediately preceding the filing of the original petition herein?
(Give the name and address of the lender, the amount of the loan and when received, the amounts and dates of payments and, if the lender is a relative or insider, the relationship.)

12. Transfers of property.

a. Have you made any gifts, other than ordinary and usual presents to family members and charitable donations, during the year immediately preceding the filing of the original petition herein? (If so, give names and addresses of donees and dates, description, and value of gifts.)

b. Have you made any other transfer, absolute or for the purpose of security, or any other disposition, of real or tangible personal property during the year immediately preceding the filing of the original petition herein? (Give a description of the property, the date of the transfer or disposition, to whom transferred or how disposed of, and, if the transferee is a relative or insider, the relationship, the consideration, if any, received therefor, and the disposition of such consideration.)

13. Repossessions and returns.

Has any property been returned to, or repossessed by, the seller or by a secured party during the year immediately preceding the filing of the original petition herein?
(If so, give particulars including the name and address of the party getting the property and its description and value.)

14. Losses.

a. Have you suffered any losses from fire, theft, or gambling during the year immediately preceding or since the filing of the original petition herein? (If so, give particulars, including dates, names, and places, and the amounts of money or value and general description of property lost.)

b. Was the loss covered in whole or part by insurance?
(If so, give particulars.)

15. Payments or transfers to attorneys.

a. Have you consulted an attorney during the year immediately preceding or since the filing of the original petition herein? (Give date, name, and address.)

b. Have you during the year immediately preceding or since the filing of the original petition herein paid any money or transferred any property to the attorney or to any other person on his behalf?
(If so, give particulars, including amount paid or value of property transferred and date of payment or transfer.)

c. Have you, either during the year immediately preceding or since the filing of the original petition herein, agreed to pay any money or transfer any property to an attorney at law, or to any other person on his behalf?
(If so, give particulars, including amount and terms of obligation.)

8a. *The answer is "No" for most individuals who file for bankruptcy.*

9. *See instructions for Form 2.*

10a. *List all pending lawsuits brought by you or against you.*

10b. *List any lawsuits that have been dismissed, or settled, or proceeded to judgment.*

10c. *If your wages have been garnished, indicate that here.*

11. *See instructions for Form 2.*

12a. *See instructions for Form 2.*

12b. *See instructions for Form 2.*

13. *If your car (or other property) has been repossessed, indicate that here. Be sure to list it as an unsecured debt on Schedule A-3.*

UNSWORN DECLARATION UNDER PENALTY OF PERJURY

I (We),   (Type name here.)   *and*

certify under penalty of perjury that I *(we)* have read the foregoing schedules, consisting of   sheets, and that they are true and correct to the best of my *(our)* knowledge, information, and belief.

Executed on   (Type in date.)   19 *(year)* ....   *(You sign here.)*

Signature   Signature

Form No. 7, statement of affairs: not engaged in business: page 2, 10-79   © 1979 JULIUS BLUMBERG, INC.

78

FORM 2, EXAMPLE, PAGE 2

8. Receiverships, general assignments, and other modes of liquidation.

    a. Was any of your property, at the time of the filing of the original petition herein, in the hands of a receiver, trustee, or other liquidating agent? (If so, give a brief description of the property, the name and address of the receiver, trustee, or other agent, and, if the agent was appointed in a court proceeding, the name and location of the court the title and number of the case, and the nature of the proceeding.)

    b. Have you made any assignment of your property for the benefit of your creditors, or any general settlement with your creditors, within one year immediately preceding the filing of the original petition herein?
(If so, give dates, the name and address of the assignee, and a brief statement of the terms of assignment or settlement.)

9. Property in hands of third person.

    Is any other person holding anything of value in which you have an interest? (Give name and address, location and description of the property, and circumstances of the holding.)

10. Suits, executions, and attachments.

    a. Were you a party to any suit pending at the time of the filing of the original petition herein? (If so, give the name and location of the court and the title and nature of the proceeding.)

    b. Were you a party to any suit terminated within the year immediately preceding the filing of the original petition herein.? (If so, give the name and location of the court, the title and nature of the proceeding, and the result.)

    c. Has any of your property been attached, garnished, or seized under any legal or equitable process within the year immediately preceding the filing of the original petition herein? (If so, describe the property seized or person garnished, and at whose suit.)

11. Loans repaid.

    What repayments on loans in whole or in part have you made during the year immediately preceding the filing of the original petition herein?
(Give the name and address of the lender, the amount of the loan and when received, the amounts and dates of payments and, if the lender is a relative or insider, the relationship.)

12. Transfers of property.

    a. Have you made any gifts, other than ordinary and usual presents to family members and charitable donations, during the year immediately preceding the filing of the original petition herein? (If so, give names and addresses of donees and dates, description, and value of gifts.)

    b. Have you made any other transfer, absolute or for the purpose of security, or any other disposition, of real or tangible personal property during the year immediately preceding the filing of the original petition herein? (Give a description of the property, the date of the transfer or disposition, to whom transferred or how disposed of, and, if the transferee is a relative or insider, the relationship, the consideration, if any, received therefor, and the disposition of such consideration.)

13. Repossessions and returns.

    Has any property been returned to, or repossessed by, the seller or by a secured party during the year immediately preceding the filing of the original petition herein?
(If so, give particulars including the name and address of the party getting the property and its description and value.)

14. Losses.

    a. Have you suffered any losses from fire, theft, or gambling during the year immediately preceding or since the filing of the original petition herein? (If so, give particulars, including dates, names, and places, and the amounts of money or value and general description of property lost.)

    b. Was the loss covered in whole or part by insurance? (If so, give particulars.)

15. Payments or transfers to attorneys.

    a. Have you consulted an attorney during the year immediately preceding or since the filing of the original petition herein? (Give date, name, and address.)

    b. Have you during the year immediately preceding or since the filing of the original petition herein paid any money or transferred any property to the attorney or to any other person on his behalf?
(If so, give particulars, including amount paid or value of property transferred and date of payment or transfer.)

    c. Have you, either during the year immediately preceding or since the filing of the original petition herein, agreed to pay any money or transfer any property to an attorney at law, or to any other person on his behalf?
(If so, give particulars, including amount and terms of obligation.)

8a. No

9. No

10a. Hilda Schwartz v. Oscar Lindstrom, San Francisco Superior Court--suit arising from auto accident.

10b. Memorial Hospital v. Oscar Lindstrom, Alameda County Municipal Court-- judgment for $925.

10c. Yes--wages by Memorial Hospital

11. Regular monthly installments to Friendly Finance

12a. No

12b. No

13. No

14a. Yes--lost $300 gambling in Reno 4/79

14b. No

15a. No

UNSWORN DECLARATION UNDER PENALTY OF PERJURY

I *(We)*,   OSCAR LINDSTROM   *and*

certify under penalty of perjury that I *(we)* have read the foregoing schedules, consisting of   sheets, and that they are true and correct to the best of my *(our)* knowledge, information, and belief.

Executed on   December 12   19 79   ....

                                      Signature   Signature

Form No. 7, statement of affairs: not engaged in business: page 2, 10-79   © 1979 JULIUS BLUMBERG, INC.

INSTRUCTIONS FOR FORM 2

Item 1b.   If you are known by a name other than your true name or initials, list that here. If you have changed your name within the last six years, whether by marriage or otherwise, put your previous name here.

Item 2d.   Get this information from your tax return or W-2 form. If you don't have a copy of your tax return, you can get one by filing Form 4506 with the Internal Revenue Service. Call the "tax information and assistance" number listed in your phone book under U.S. Government and ask them to mail you a copy of this form.

Item 2e.   This might include interest on bank accounts, dividends, child or spousal support from a prior marriage, public benefits, Social Security, veterans' benefits, and so on. Again, the information should match up with your tax returns.

Item 3c.   If you haven't filed your tax returns yet, type in "Unknown." But remember, you may lose the refund to the trustee (see Chapter 7).

Item 4a.   List the name and address of the financial institution and the account number for any accounts you have had at a bank, savings and loan association, credit union, or other financial institution. Be sure to list any accounts you may have closed in anticipation of bankruptcy.

Item 9.   This includes landlords and utility companies that hold deposits for you.

Remember that it is not worthwhile to ask your friends or relatives to hide any of your property for you. You risk losing that all-important discharge from debt.

Item 11.   Do not pay off debts to friends or relatives on the eve of bankruptcy—they will just have to give the money to the trustee.

If you made payments on any loans, list them here. You can simply type in "Regular monthly payments" if that is the case.

Item 12a. Do not try to save nonexempt property by giving it away—it doesn't work. Your friends will just have to give the money to the trustee.

Item 12b. If you sold any property—perhaps to convert the proceeds into exempt property—indicate that here. Also, if you have borrowed any money and agreed that any of your property — like household goods — was security for the loan, indicate that here.

NOTE. Form 2 is designed for a debtor who is not engaged in business. If you are conducting your own business as a sole proprietor, you must complete a variation of this form entitled "Statement of Financial Affairs for Debtor Engaged in Business." Copies of this form are available at most stationery stores.

If you are conducting your own business as a partnership, you may file for straight bankruptcy. However, before you do so, you should consult an attorney to discuss the impact of your bankruptcy filing on you, your business, and your partners.

If you are conducting your own business as a corporation, either you or your corporation or both may file for bankruptcy. The choice can be a complicated one. Consult an attorney before making any decision.

UNITED STATES BANKRUPTCY COURT FOR THE *See instruction 1,* **DISTRICT OF** *Type in the name of your state.* **Case No.**

Form 1

In re *See instruction 2, Form 1*

Schedule A — STATEMENT OF ALL LIABILITIES OF DEBTOR

Debtor   Include here all named used by debtor within last 6 years.

(If this form is used by joint debtors wherever the word "debtor" or words referring to debtor are used they shall be read as if in the plural.)

Schedules A-1, A-2, and A-3 must include all the claims against the debtor(s) or debtors' property as of the date of the filing of the petition by or against debtor.

SCHEDULE A-1 — CREDITORS HAVING PRIORITY

(1) Nature of Claim	(2) Name of creditor and complete mailing address including zip code (if unknown, so state)	(3) Specify when claim was incurred and the consideration therefor; when claim is contingent, unliquidated, disputed, or subject to setoff, evidenced by a judgment, negotiable instrument, or other writing, or incurred as partner or joint contractor, so indicate; specify name of any partner or joint contractor on any debt.	(4) Indicate if claim is contingent, unliquidated or disputed.	(5) Amount of Claim
a. Wages, salary, and commissions, including vacation, severance and sick leave pay owing to workmen, servants, clerks, or traveling or city salesmen on salary or commission basis, whole or part time, whether or not selling exclusively for the debtor, not exceeding $2,000 to each, earned within 90 days before filing of petition or cessation of business, if earlier (specify date).	*Entries in a, b, or c are rare for consumer debtors.*			$
b. Contributions to employee benefit plans for services rendered within 180 days before filing of petition or cessation of business, if earlier (specify date).				
c. Deposits by individuals, not exceeding $900 for each for purchase, lease, or rental of property or services for personal, family, or household use that were not delivered or provided.				
d. Taxes owing (itemize by type of tax and taxing authority:) (1) To the United States (2) To any State (3) To any other taxing authority	*List here any taxes owed to the state or federal government on income you earned in prior years.*			
			Total	

Form No. 6, Schedule A-1, 10-79

© 1979 JULIUS BLUMBERG, INC.

UNITED STATES BANKRUPTCY COURT FOR THE **NORTHERN** DISTRICT OF **CALIFORNIA**   *Case No.*

In re   OSCAR LINDSTROM
       aka RED LINDSTROM

Schedule A — STATEMENT OF ALL LIABILITIES OF DEBTOR

Debtor   Include here all named used by debtor within last 6 years.

(If this form is used by joint debtors wherever the word "debtor" or words referring to debtor are used they shall be read as if in the plural.)
Schedules A-1, A-2, and A-3 must include all the claims against the debtor(s) or debtors' property as of the date of the filing of the petition by or against debtor.

SCHEDULE A-1 — CREDITORS HAVING PRIORITY

(1) Nature of Claim	(2) Name of creditor and complete mailing address including zip code (if unknown, so state)	(3) Specify when claim was incurred and the consideration therefor; when claim is contingent, unliquidated, disputed, or subject to setoff, evidenced by a judgment, negotiable instrument, or other writing, or incurred as partner or joint contractor, so indicate; specify name of any partner or joint contractor on any debt.	(4) Indicate if claim is contingent, unliquidated or disputed.	(5) Amount of Claim
a. Wages, salary, and commissions, including vacation, severance and sick leave pay owing to workmen, servants, clerks, or traveling or city salesmen on salary or commission basis, whole or part time, whether or not selling exclusively for the debtor, not exceeding $2,000 to each, earned within 90 days before filing of petition or cessation of business, if earlier (specify date).	None			$
b. Contributions to employee benefit plans for services rendered within 180 days before filing of petition or cessation of business, if earlier (specify date).	None			
c. Deposits by individuals, not exceeding $900 for each for purchase, lease, or rental of property or services for personal, family, or household use that were not delivered or provided.	None			
d. Taxes owing (itemize by type of tax and taxing authority:) (1) To the United States (2) To any State (3) To any other taxing authority	None			
			Total	

Form No. 6, Schedule A-1, 10-79

© 1979 JULIUS BLUMBERG, INC.

FORM 3, PAGE 2

Schedule A-2 — Creditors Holding Security

(1) Name of creditor and complete mailing address including zip code (if unknown, so state)	(2) Description of security and date when obtained by creditor	(3) Specify when claim was incurred and the consideration therefor; when claim is contingent, unliquidated, disputed, subject to setoff, evidenced by a judgment, negotiable instrument, or other writing, or incurred as partner or joint contractor, so indicate; specify name of any partner or joint contractor on any debt.	(4) Indicate if claim is contingent, unliquidated or disputed	(5) Market value	(6) Amount of claim without deduction of value of security
				$	$
List the name and address of each of your secured creditors in alphabetical order. See Chapter 5, Step 3 to determine which debts are secured. Be sure to indicate in column 4 if the existence or the amount of a debt is disputed or uncertain. Entries in this column will be rare. List the present value of the secured property in column 5, given its age and present condition — not what you paid for it. List the unpaid balance on the debt in column 6.					

None of the above claims is contingent, liquidated or disputed unless otherwise stated. **Total**

Schedule A-3 — Creditors Having Unsecured Claims Without Priority

Name of creditor (including last known holder of any negotiable instrument) complete mailing address including zip code (if unknown, so state).	Specify when claim was incurred and the consideration therefor; when claim is contingent, unliquidated, disputed, subject to setoff, evidenced by a judgment, negotiable instrument, or other writing, or incurred as partner or joint contractor, so indicate; specify name of any partner or joint contractor on any debt.	Amount of Claim
		$

List the name and address of each of your unsecured creditors here in alphabetical order. Remember to include
   1. collection agencies or attorneys who have contacted you about debts,
   2. people who cosigned loans for you,
   3. debts you cosigned for others.
   4. guarantors of student loans, and
   5. debts for items that have been repossessed.
 	
Thus, if you borrowed money from A and then got dunning letters from collection agency B followed by calls from attorney C, you would list A, B, and C here.
 	
It is very important that you list everything — even those debts you dispute or intend to pay. Check this list against your worksheets. Be sure that all of your debts are listed somewhere in Schedules A-1, A-2, and A-3.		

None of the above claims is contingent, liquidated or disputed unless otherwise stated. **Total**

Form No. 6, Schedule A-2 & A-3, 10-79 .

© 1979 JULIUS BLUMBERG, INC.

FORM 3, EXAMPLE, PAGE 2

Schedule A-2 — Creditors Holding Security

(1) Name of creditor and complete mailing address including zip code (if unknown, so state)	(2) Description of security and date when obtained by creditor	(3) Specify when claim was incurred and the consideration therefor; when claim is contingent, unliquidated, disputed, subject to setoff, evidenced by a judgment, negotiable instrument, or other writing, or incurred as partner or joint contractor, so indicate; specify name of any partner or joint contractor on any debt.	(4) Indicate if claim is contingent, unliquidated or disputed	(5) Market value	(6) Amount of claim without deduction of value of security
Fred's Appliance Store, 82 Fifth Avenue, San Francisco CA 94102. Security interest in television set purchased 10/78.				$ 200.	$ 400.
Friendly Finance, 318 Kansas Street, San Francisco CA 94109. Security interest in household goods. Vacation loan, contract entered 3/77.				800.	1,800.
State Bank, 1011 Maple Street, Oakland CA 94703. Security interest in 1974 Chevrolet Malibu. Automobile financing, contract entered 9/75.				1,500.	1,100.
None of the above claims is contingent, liquidated or disputed unless otherwise stated.			Total	2,500.	3,300.

Schedule A-3 — Creditors Having Unsecured Claims Without Priority

Name of creditor (including last known holder of any negotiable instrument) complete mailing address including zip code (if unknown, so state).	Specify when claim was incurred and the consideration therefor; when claim is contingent, unliquidated, disputed, subject to setoff, evidenced by a judgment, negotiable instrument, or other writing, or incurred as partner or joint contractor, so indicate; specify name of any partner or joint contractor on any debt.	Amount of Claim
Bancocard, 4129 Montgomery Street, Hartford CT 06103. Miscellaneous purchases. 6/76 to date.		$ 970.
Big Man Health Club, 807 Poplar Lane, South San Francisco CA 94111. For membership 10/78.		980.
City Utility Company, 10321 Mission Street, San Francisco CA 94104. Utility services 11/79.		80.
Driveon Oil Company, 777 Sunset Lane, Los Angeles CA 90023. For gas 1/79 to date.		240.
County of Erehwon, 110 Court Street, Erehwon NV 89503. Traffic tickets 4/79.		110.
Hammero Collection Agency, 811 Main Street, Oakland CA 94703. Collecting for Wearforever Clothes.		Duplicate
Anna Lindstrom, 18 Solomon Street, Whittier CA 90605. Spousal support and child support 1/77 to present.		700.
Inez Lindstrom, 789 Ocean View, San Francisco CA 94115. Cosigned loan to Friendly Finance 3/77.		Duplicate
None of the above claims is contingent, liquidated or disputed unless otherwise stated.	Total	3,080.

Form No. 6, Schedule A-2 & A-3, 10-79

© 1979 JULIUS BLUMBERG. INC.

Schedule A-3 — Creditors Having Unsecured Claims Without Priority

Name of creditor (including last known holder of any negotiable instrument) complete mailing address including zip code (if unknown, so state).	Specify when claim was incurred and the consideration therefor; when claim is contingent, unliquidated, disputed, subject to setoff, evidenced by a judgment, negotiable instrument, or other writing, or incurred as partner or joint contractor, so indicate; specify name of any partner or joint contractor on any debt	Amount of claim
		$

Continue listing your unsecured debts here. Be sure to indicate if the existence of the amount of a debt is disputed or uncertain (for example, liability arising from an auto accident before the litigation is concluded).

None of the above claims is contingent, liquidated or disputed unless otherwise stated.　　　　Total

Form No. 6, Schedule A-3, 10-79

© 1979 JULIUS BLUMBERG, INC.

Schedule A-3 — Creditors Having Unsecured Claims Without Priority

Name of creditor (including last known holder of any negotiable instrument) complete mailing address including zip code (if unknown, so state).	Specify when claim was incurred and the consideration therefor; when claim is contingent, unliquidated, disputed, subject to setoff, evidenced by a judgment, negotiable instrument, or other writing, or incurred as partner or joint contractor, so indicate; specify name of any partner or joint contractor on any debt	Amount of claim
		$
Otto Lindstrom, 18 State Street, Bakersfield CA 93302. Personal loan 2/78.		250.
Memorial Hospital, 358 Ashby Avenue, Berkeley CA 94705. Medical care 10/79; evidenced by judgment.		925.
Jack T. Ragoon, Attorney at Law, 440 Ashby Avenue, Berkeley CA 94705. Collection for Memorial Hospital.		Duplicate
Hilda Schwartz, 3811 Rose Street, San Leandro CA 92068. Auto accident 8/79; claim disputed and unliquidated.		1,600.
Truvalo University, 311 Yale Avenue, Berkeley CA 94708. Student loans 9/72-9/75.		3,000.
Dr. Charles Tyler, 322 Ashby Avenue, Berkeley CA 94705. Medical care 10/79.		280.
Wearforever Clothes Store, 308 San Pablo, Richmond CA 94539. Clothes 2/79-9/79.		310.
None of the above claims is contingent, liquidated or disputed unless otherwise stated.	Total	6,365.

Form No. 6, Schedule A-3, 10-79

© 1979 JULIUS BLUMBERG, INC.

FORM 4, PAGE 1

SCHEDULE B — STATEMENT OF ALL PROPERTY OF DEBTOR

Schedules B-1, B-2, B-3, and B-4 must include all property of the debtor as of the date of the filing of the petition by or against debtor.

Schedule B-1 — Real Property

Description and location of all real property in which debtor has an interest (including equitable and future interests, interests in estates by the entirety, community property, life estates, lease-holds, and rights and powers exercisable for the benefit of debtor)	Nature of interest (specify all deeds and written instruments relating thereto)	Market value of debtor's interest without deduction for secured claims listed in schedule A-2 or exemptions claimed in schedule B-4	
If you own a home or other real property, list it here.		$	
	Total		

Schedule B-2 — Personal Property

Type of Property	Description and location	Market value of debtor's interest without deduction for secured claims listed on schedule A-2 or exemptions claimed in schedule B-4	
a. Cash on hand	a. *Any cash on hand must be turned over to the trustee unless you claim federal exemption 16.*	$	
b. Deposits of money with banking institutions, savings and loan associations, credit unions, public utility companies, landlords, and others	b. *Be careful with these, too, if you claim the state exemptions.*		
c. Household goods, supplies, and furnishings			
d. Books, pictures, and other art objects; stamp, coin, and other collections	*List all your property — item by item — in the category that best describes it. Double check your list against your worksheet. All of your property should be listed somewhere in Schedules B-1, B-2, or B-3.*		
e. Wearing apparel, jewelry, firearms, sports equipment, and other personal possessions			
f. Automobiles, trucks, trailers, and other vehicles	*List the present value, given the property's age, and present condition in the last column. List your car at low Blue Book.*		
g. Boats, motors, and their accessories			
	Total		

Form No. 6. Schedule B-1 & B-2. 10-79

© 1979 JULIUS BLUMBERG, INC.

FORM 4, EXAMPLE, PAGE 1

SCHEDULE B — STATEMENT OF ALL PROPERTY OF DEBTOR

Schedules B-1, B-2, B-3, and B-4 must include all property of the debtor as of the date of the filing of the petition by or against debtor.

Schedule B-1 — Real Property

Description and location of all real property in which debtor has an interest (including equitable and future interests, interests in estates by the entirety, community property, life estates, lease-holds, and rights and powers exercisable for the benefit of debtor)	Nature of interest (specify all deeds and written instruments relating thereto)	Market value of debtor's interest without deduction for secured claims listed in schedule A-2 or exemptions claimed in schedule B-4
None		$
Total		–0–

Schedule B-2 — Personal Property

Type of Property	Description and location	Market value of debtor's interest without deduction for secured claims listed on schedule A-2 or exemptions claimed in schedule B-4
a. Cash on hand		$
b. Deposits of money with banking institutions, savings and loan associations, credit unions, public utility companies, landlords, and others	b. American Bank, 33 Main Street, San Francisco CA. Christmas Club account number 35821	120.
	Checking account number 6219758	350.
	Savings account number 531-0928	475.
c. Household goods, supplies, and furnishings	c. Stereo at my residence	300.
	Couch " " "	100.
	Bed " " "	75.
d. Books, pictures, and other art objects; stamp, coin, and other collections	Chest " " "	20.
	Breakfast Set "	60.
	Kitchen Goods "	45.
	Television "	200.
e. Wearing apparel, jewelry, firearms, sports equipment, and other personal possessions	d. Coin collection"	175.
	e. Wearing Apparel"	100.
	Golf Clubs "	100.
	Power Tools "	150.
f. Automobiles, trucks, trailers, and other vehicles	f. 1974 Chevrolet Malibu, license No. 021VHZ	1,500.
g. Boats, motors, and their accessories		
	Total	3,770.

Form No. 6, Schedule B-1 & B-2, 10-79

© 1979 JULIUS BLUMBERG, INC

Schedule B-2 — Personal Property (Continued)

Type of property	Description and location	Market value of debtor's interest without deduction for secured claims listed on schedule A-2 or exemptions claimed in schedule B-4	
h. Livestock, poultry, and other animals		$	
i. Farming supplies and implements			
j. Office equipment, furnishings, and supplies			
k. Machinery, fixtures, equipment, and supplies (other than those listed in items j and l) used in business	*List the tools of your trade here.*		
l. Inventory			
m. Tangible personal property of any other description			
n. Patents, copyrights, franchises, and other general intangibles (specify all documents and writings relating thereto)			
o. Government and corporate bonds and other negotiable and nonnegotiable instruments	*List U. S. Savings Bonds here.*		
p. Other liquidated debts owing debtor	*List wages due here. See Chapter 7 on how to make wages exempt.*		
q. Contingent and unliquidated claims of every nature, including counterclaims of the debtor (give estimated value of each)			
r. Interests in insurance policies (itemize surrender or refund values of each)	*Be sure to list all policies — health, fire, auto, life, disability, and group insurance through your employer.*		
s. Annuities			
t. Stocks and interests in incorporated and unincorporated companies (itemize separately)			
u. Interests in partnerships			
v. Equitable and future interests, life estates, and rights or powers exercisable for the benefit of the debtor (other than those listed in schedule B-1) [specify all written instruments relating thereto]		Total	

Schedule B-2 — Personal Property (Continued)

Type of property	Description and location	Market value of debtor's interest without deduction for secured claims listed on schedule A-2 or exemptions claimed in schedule B-4
h. Livestock, poultry, and other animals		$
i. Farming supplies and implements		
j. Office equipment, furnishings, and supplies		
k. Machinery, fixtures, equipment, and supplies (other than those listed in items j and l) used in business	Mower, rake, hoe, shovel, clippers (tools of trade) at my residence	180.
l. Inventory		
m. Tangible personal property of any other description		
n. Patents, copyrights, franchises, and other general intangibles (specify all documents and writings relating thereto)		
o. Government and corporate bonds and other negotiable and nonnegotiable instruments	U.S. Savings Bonds at my residence 1x$50 E 8729643 1x$50 E 1023579 1x$50 E 1283521 1x$50 E 1436947 1x$50 E 1682136	250.
p. Other liquidated debts owing debtor		
q. Contingent and unliquidated claims of every nature, including counterclaims of the debtor (give estimated value of each)	Earned but unpaid wages	Unknown
r. Interests in insurance policies (itemize surrender or refund values of each)	Life insurance--Prudent Equity Company 3811 Hall Street, Hartford CT 21469 Policy number 32891	700.
s. Annuities		
t. Stocks and interests in incorporated and unincorporated companies (itemize separately)		
u. Interests in partnerships		
v. Equitable and future interests, life estates, and rights or powers exercisable for the benefit of the debtor (other than those listed in schedule B-1) [specify all written instruments relating thereto]	Total	1,130.

Form No. 6, Schedule B-2 (Continued), 10-79

© 1979 JULIUS BLUMBERG, INC.

FORM 4, PAGE 3

Schedule B-3 — Property Not Otherwise Scheduled

Type of property	Description and location	Market value of debtor's interest without deduction for secured claims listed in schedule A-2 or exemptions claimed in schedule B-4
a. Property transferred under assignment for benefit of creditors, within 120 days prior to filing of petition (specify date of assignment, name and address of assignee, amount realized therefrom by the assignee, and disposition, of proceeds so far as known to debtor)	*Most people will leave this blank. It should match up with your answer to Question 8, Statement of Affairs (Form 2, page 2)*	$
b. Property of any kind not otherwise scheduled		
	If you picked the Federal Exemption System, check the first box. *If you picked the State Exemption System, check the second box and type in the name of your state.*	
	Total	

Debtor selects the following property as exempt pursuant to ☐ 11 U.S.C. §522(d)
☐ the laws of the State of ....

Schedule B-4 — Property Claimed as Exempt

Type of property	Location, description, and so far as relevant to the claim of exemption, present use of property	Specify statute creating the exemption	Value claimed exempt
List your exempt assets here. Double check the information you list here against (1) your worksheet contained in Chapter 7 and (2) the information you filled in on Schedules B-1, B-2, and B-3 (Form 4, pages 1-3). If you need more room, continue on a blank piece of paper.		*The statutes are listed after each exemption in Chapter 7.*	$
		Total	

FORM 4, EXAMPLE, PAGE 4

Schedule B-3 — Property Not Otherwise Scheduled

Type of property	Description and location	Market value of debtor's interest without deduction for secured claims listed in schedule A-2 or exemptions claimed in schedule B-4
a. Property transferred under assignment for benefit of creditors, within 120 days prior to filing of petition (specify date of assignment, name and address of assignee, amount realized therefrom by the assignee, and disposition, of proceeds so far as known to debtor)		$
b. Property of any kind not otherwise scheduled		
	Total	-0-

Debtor selects the following property as exempt pursuant to ☒ 11 U.S.C. §522(d)
 ☐ the laws of the State of...

Schedule B-4 — Property Claimed as Exempt

Type of property	Location, description, and so far as relevant to the claim of exemption, present use of property	Specify statute creating the exemption	Value claimed exempt
			$
1974 Chevrolet Malibu	At my residence	11 USC 522 (d)(2) and (d)(5)	1,500.
Bank accounts at American Bank 33 Main Street, San Francisco CA		11 USC 522 (d)(5)	
Christmas Club account no. 35821			120.
Checking account no. 6219758			350.
Savings account no. 531-0928			475.
U.S. Savings Bonds		11 USC 522 (d)(5)	250.
1x$50 E 8729643			
1x$50 E 1023579			
1x$50 E 1283521			
1x$50 E 1436947			
1x$50 E 1682136		11 USC 522 (d)(5)	
Earned but unpaid wages from Acme Garden Company, 238 Fulton, San Francisco CA.			Unknown
		Total	2,695.

If you have more exempt assets than you can fit on the bottom of Form 4, page 3, under "Property Claimed as Exempt," continue listing them on a blank sheet of paper, as in the Example on the next page.

Additional Page to Schedule B-4
Bankruptcy of Oscar Lindstrom

Life insurance--Prudent Equity Company No. 32891	11 USC 522 (d) (8)	$700
Power Tools	At my residence	11 USC 522 (d) (5)	150
Golf Clubs	" "	11 USC 522 (d) (5)	100
Coin Collection	" "	11 USC 522 (d) (5)	175
Wearing Apparel	" "	11 USC 522 (d) (3)	100
Stereo	" "	11 USC 522 (d) (3) and (d) (5)	300
Couch	" "	11 USC 522 (d) (3)	100
Bed	" "	11 USC 522 (d) (3)	75
Chest	" "	11 USC 522 (d) (3)	20
Breakfast Set	" "	11 USC 522 (d) (3)	60
Kitchen Goods	" "	11 USC 522 (d) (3)	45
Television	" "	11 USC 522 (d) (3)	200
Mower, rake, hoe shovel, clippers	" "	11 USC 522 (d) (6)	180

Total: 2,205

FORM 4, PAGE 5

SUMMARY OF DEBTS AND PROPERTY

(From the statements of the debtor in Schedule A and B)

Schedule   Total

DEBTS

Type in the total from the →
bottom of each schedule.

A—1/a, b.................Wages, etc. having priority..
A—1(c).................Deposits of money...
A—1/(d)1.................Taxes owing United States.................................
A—1/(d)2.................Taxes owing states..
A—1/(d)3.................Taxes owing other taxing authorities.................
A—2.................Secured claims..
A—3.................Unsecured claims without priority.......................

Schedule A total

PROPERTY

Add up the total →
from each category of
property on Schedule B.

B—1.................Real property (total value).................................
B—2/a.................Cash on hand..
B—2/b.................Deposits ....
B—2/c.................Household goods...
B—2/d.................Books, pictures, and collections.......................
B—2/e.................Wearing apparel and personal possessions.......
B—2/f.................Automobiles and other vehicles.......................
B—2/g.................Boats, motors, and accessories........................
B—2/h.................Livestock and other animals............................
B—2/i.................Farming supplies and implements....................
B—2/j.................Office equipment and supplies.......................
B—2/k.................Machinery, equipment, and supplies used in business..
B—2/l.................Inventory...
B—2/m.................Other tangible personal property.....................
B—2/n.................Patents and other general intangibles.............
B—2/o.................Bonds and other instruments.........................
B—2/p.................Other liquidated debts...................................
B—2/q.................Contingent and unliquidated claims.................
B—2/r.................Interests in insurance policies.......................
B—2/s.................Annuities..
B—2/t.................Interests in corporations and unincorporated companies..
B—2/u.................Interests in partnerships................................
B—2/v.................Equitable and future interests, rights, and powers in personalty..
B—3/a.................Property assigned for benefit of creditors.......
B—3/b.................Property not otherwise scheduled....................

Schedule B total

UNSWORN DECLARATION UNDER PENALTY OF PERJURY

INDIVIDUAL(S): I(we)   *(Fill in your name)*   *and*

certify under penalty of perjury that I(we) have read the foregoing schedules, consisting of   sheets, and that they are true and
correct to the best of my(our) knowledge, information, and belief.   *(Fill in the number of pages.)*

CORPORATION: I,   the *(insert president or other officer or an authorized agent)*
                                                         of the corporation named as debtor in this case, certify under penalty
of perjury that I have read the foregoing schedules, consisting of   sheets, and that they are true and correct to the best of my
knowledge, information, and belief.

PARTNERSHIP: I,   a *(insert member or an authorized agent)*
                                                         of the partnership named as debtor in this case, certify under penalty
of perjury that I have read the foregoing schedules, consisting of   sheets, and that they are true and correct to the best of my
knowledge, information, and belief.

Executed on   *(Fill in the date.)*   19 ....   *(You sign here.)*
                                                         ....
                                                              Signature   Signature

Form 6, Summary of debts & property, declarations.

© 1979 JULIUS BLUMBERG, INC.

SUMMARY OF DEBTS AND PROPERTY (From the statements of the debtor in Schedule A and B)

Schedule		Total

DEBTS

Schedule	Description	Total
A—1/a, b	Wages, etc. having priority	
A—1(c)	Deposits of money	
A—1/(d)1	Taxes owing United States	
A—1/(d)2	Taxes owing states	
A—1/(d)3	Taxes owing other taxing authorities	
A—2	Secured claims	3,300
A—3	Unsecured claims without priority	9,445
	Schedule A total	12,745

PROPERTY

Schedule	Description	Total
B—1	Real property (total value)	
B—2/a	Cash on hand	945
B—2/b	Deposits	800
B—2/c	Household goods	175
B—2/d	Books, pictures, and collections	350
B—2/e	Wearing apparel and personal possessions	
B—2/f	Automobiles and other vehicles	1,500
B—2/g	Boats, motors, and accessories	
B—2/h	Livestock and other animals	
B—2/i	Farming supplies and implements	
B—2/j	Office equipment and supplies	
B—2/k	Machinery, equipment, and supplies used in business	180
B—2/l	Inventory	
B—2/m	Other tangible personal property	
B—2/n	Patents and other general intangibles	
B—2/o	Bonds and other instruments	250
B—2/p	Other liquidated debts	
B—2/q	Contingent and unliquidated claims	unknown
B—2/r	Interests in insurance policies	700
B—2/s	Annuities	
B—2/t	Interests in corporations and unincorporated companies	
B—2/u	Interests in partnerships	
B—2/v	Equitable and future interests, rights, and powers in personalty	
B—3/a	Property assigned for benefit of creditors	
B—3/b	Property not otherwise scheduled	
	Schedule B total	4,900

UNSWORN DECLARATION UNDER PENALTY OF PERJURY

INDIVIDUAL(S): I*(we)* OSCAR LINDSTROM   *and*
certify under penalty of perjury that I*(we)* have read the foregoing schedules, consisting of   7   sheets, and that they are true and correct to the best of my*(our)* knowledge, information, and belief.

CORPORATION: I,   the *(insert president or other officer or an authorized agent)*
                                                                                          of the corporation named as debtor in this case, certify under penalty
of perjury that I have read the foregoing schedules, consisting of   sheets, and that they are true and correct to the best of my
knowledge, information, and belief.

PARTNERSHIP: I,   a *(insert member or an authorized agent)*
                                                                                          of the partnership named as debtor in this case, certify under penalty
of perjury that I have read the foregoing schedules, consisting of   sheets, and that they are true and correct to the best of my
knowledge, information, and belief.

Executed on   December 12   19 79   *Oscar Lindstrom*
                                                                       Signature   Signature

Form 6, Summary of debts & property, declarations.   © 1979 JULIUS BLUMBERG, INC.

FORM 5

BANKRUPT NAME & ADDRESS	ATTORNEY(S) NAME & ADDRESS	BANKRUPT/DEBTOR NO.

DISTRICT DIRECTOR INTERNAL REVENUE SERVICE DISTRICT OFFICE ADDRESS	START A-Z LIST OF CREDITORS	

Type in the name and address of each of your creditors in alphabetical order. Be sure to list all of those included on Schedule A. Double check to make sure the names and addresses are correct.

DO NOT TYPE IN THIS AREA

If a debt is disclosed to the United States other than one for taxes, type an address for the United States Attorney for the district in which the case is pending and to the department, agent or instrumentality of the United States through which the bankrupt became indebted.

Check with your local district for addresses of state or local government agencies to which addressed label must be prepared.

© 1973 BY JULIUS BLUMBERG, INC.,

FORM 5, EXAMPLE

BANKRUPT NAME & ADDRESS	ATTORNEY(S) NAME & ADDRESS	BANKRUPT/DEBTOR NO.
Oscar Lindstrom 538 Mission St. San Francisco, CA 94104		
DISTRICT DIRECTOR **INTERNAL REVENUE SERVICE** **DISTRICT OFFICE ADDRESS**	**START A-Z LIST OF CREDITORS**	
Bancocard 4129 Montgomery Street Hartford CT 06103	Anna Lindstrom 18 Solomon Street Whittier CA 90605	Dr. Charles Tyler 322 Ashby Avenue Berkeley CA 94705
Big Man Health Club 807 Poplar Lane San Francisco CA 94111	Inez Lindstrom 789 Ocean View San Francisco CA 94115	Wearforever Clothes Store 309 San Pablo Richmond CA 94539
City Utility Company 10321 Mission Street San Francisco CA 94104	Otto Lindstrom 18 State Street Bakersfield CA 80236	
Driveon Gas Company 777 Sunset Lane Los Angeles CA 62841	Memorial Hospital 358 Ashby Avenue Berkeley CA 94705	
County of Erehwon 110 Court Street Erehwon NV 89503	Jack Ragoon Attorney at Law 440 Ashby Avenue Berkeley CA 94705	
Fred's Appliance Store 82 Fifth Avenue San Francisco CA 94102	Hilda Schwartz 3811 Rose Street San Leandro CA 92608	
Friendly Finance 318 Kansas Street San Francisco 94109	State Bank 1011 Maple Street Oakland CA 94703	
Hammero Collection Agy. 811 Main Street Oakland CA 94703	Truvalo University 311 Yale Avenue Berkeley CA 94708	

DO NOT TYPE IN THIS AREA

If a debt is disclosed to the United States other than one for taxes, type an address for the United States Attorney for the district in which the case is pending and to the department, agent or instrumentality of the United States through which the bankrupt became indebted.

Check with your local district for addresses of state or local government agencies to which addressed label must be prepared.

© 1973 BY JULIUS BLUMBERG, INC.,

RECHECKING YOUR WORK

Now that your forms are complete, it's time to recheck them carefully. Make sure the information on your worksheets agrees with what you typed on the bankruptcy forms. If you have any unanswered questions, see a lawyer.

SIGNING AND FILING YOUR FORMS

Sign Form 1, Form 2, page 2, and Form 4, page 5, and make four copies of each. You must file the original and three copies of each form with the clerk of the bankruptcy court. The fourth copy is for you to keep for your records.

Take the five sets of forms (the original and four copies), together with the filing fee — $60 in cash — to the clerk of the bankruptcy court in your judicial district.

You "file" for bankruptcy by handing the five sets of forms and $60 in cash to the clerk. The clerk will give you a receipt and return to you one full set of forms marked "filed" with the date in the upper right hand corner and stamped with the number of your case on each form.

It is also possible to file by mail. Instead of sending cash, enclose a $60 money order payable to the U.S. Bankruptcy Clerk. It is preferable to file in person so that you will have the opportunity to clear up any questions you may have about filing papers or how things are handled in court. Bankruptcy clerks can be very helpful with these matters, but their ability to assist you with any other questions you may have is quite limited. In particular, they are not allowed to give legal advice — they are not attorneys, and it would be illegal for them to do so.

CHAPTER

$$\$\$\$\$\$$

THE MEETING OF CREDITORS

As soon as you have filed for bankruptcy, you can enjoy a bit of a breathing spell as you will not have to attend the meeting of creditors for approximately four to six weeks. If your wages are being attached or money is being taken out of your paycheck for your credit union, notify your employers right away so that they can stop making those deductions from your paycheck. Take a copy of your bankruptcy petition (Form 1) to the sheriff and the credit union so they will know to stop asking for the automatic deductions. Stop paying your dischargeable debts. Don't worry about your creditors. The court will notify each of them of your pending bankruptcy action. You don't have to do it. Upon notification, they must immediately stop all harassment, bill-collection efforts, wage garnishments, lawsuits, foreclosures, and repossessions. If any of your creditors should contact you in the week or so between your filing and their notification by the court, simply tell them of your bankruptcy filing and give them the number the clerk put on the first page of your bankruptcy papers. If they don't believe you, tell them to call the bankruptcy court. If your creditors persist, you may wind up having grounds to sue them!

Within a week or two of filing, you and your creditors will each receive in the mail from the court a Notice of Meeting of Creditors. It will probably look something like Form 6.

Form 6

UNITED STATES BANKRUPTCY COURT
FOR THE NORTHERN DISTRICT OF CALIFORNIA

IN RE   OSCAR LINDSTROM
aka RED LINDSTROM

Debtor   Bankruptcy No. 158259

ORDER FOR MEETING OF CREDITORS AND FIXING TIMES
FOR FILING OBJECTIONS TO DISCHARGE AND FOR FIL-
ING COMPLAINTS TO DETERMINE DISCHARGEABILITY
OF CERTAIN DEBTS, COMBINED WITH NOTICE THEREOF
AND OF AUTOMATIC STAY

To the debtor, his creditors, and other parties in interest:

An order for relief under 11 U.S.C. chapter 7 having been entered on a petition filed by *Oscar Lindstrom* of *538 Mission Street, San Francisco CA 94104*, on *December 12, 1979*, it is ordered, and notice is hereby given that:

1. A meeting of creditors pursuant to 11 U.S.C. § 341(a) shall be held at *Room 17435, Federal Building and U.S. Courthouse, 450 Golden Gate Avenue, San Francisco CA* on *January 10, 1980* at *10* o'clock *a*.m.

2. The debtor shall appear in person at that time and place for the purpose of being examined.

3. *April 10, 1980* is fixed as the last day for the filing of objections to the discharge of the debtor.

4. *April 10, 1980* is fixed as the last day for the filing of a complaint to determine the dischargeability of any debt pursuant to 11 U.S.C. § 523(c).

You are further notified that:

The meeting may be continued or adjourned from time to time by notice at the meeting, without further written notice to creditors.

At the meeting the creditors may file their claims, elect a trustee as permitted by law, designate a person to supervise the meeting, elect a committee of creditors, examine the debtor, and transact such other business as may properly come before the meeting.

As a result of the filing of the petition, certain acts and proceedings against the debtor and his property are stayed as provided in 11 U.S.C. § 362(a).

If no objection to the discharge of the debtor is filed on or before the last day fixed therefor as stated in subparagraph 3 above, the debtor will be granted his discharge. If no complaint to determine the dischargeability of a debt under clause (2), (4), or (6) of 11 U.S.C. § 523(a) is filed within the time fixed therefore as stated in subparagraph 4 above, the debt may be discharged.

It appears from the schedules of the debtor that there are no assets from which any dividend can be paid to creditors. It is unnecessary for any creditor to file a claim at this time in order to share in any distribution from the estate. If it subsequently appears that there are assets from which a dividend may be paid, creditors will be so notified and given an opportunity to file their claims.

Unless the court extends the time, any objection to the debtor's claim of exempt property (Schedule B-4) must be filed within 15 days after the above date set for the meeting of creditors.

THE MEETING OF CREDITORS

Walter Neilson of 2138 Van Ness Avenue, San Francisco CA 94111 has been appointed interim trustee of the estate of the above-named debtor.

IT IS ORDERED, AND NOTICE IS HEREBY GIVEN that:

1. Discharge hearing pursuant to 11 U.S.C. § 524(d) will be held at *Room 17435, Federal Building and United States Courthouse, 450 Golden Gate Avenue, San Francisco, CA,* on *April 25, 1980,* at *10* o'clock a.m.

2. The debtor(s) shall appear, with their attorneys of record, at the time and place hereinabove set forth.

3. Motions for approval of reaffirmation agreements of the kind specified in 11 U.S.C. § 524(d) must be filed at least ten days prior to the discharge hearing and will be heard and determined at that hearing.

Dated   December 16, 1979
_____

BY THE COURT

_____ ,
Bankruptcy Judge

You *must* attend the meeting of creditors. If it is really impossible for you to do so, call the clerk in advance and arrange another date.

The meeting itself won't take very long — it could be as short as five minutes. But a number of other debtors will have been summoned for meetings at the same time, so it is safe to guess that you may have to wait your turn for an hour or so. That's all right — it will give you a chance to get your bearings.

When your name is called, step to the front of the room. A clerk will have you raise your right hand and swear that everything you are about to say will be the truth. A court reporter will take down everything that is said with a transcribing machine.

At a typical meeting of creditors, the trustee might ask the following questions:

1. What is your name?
2. Do you still live at (the address listed on the Petition)?
3. Do you rent where you live?
4. Are you married?
5. What is your home phone number?
6. Have you ever filed for bankruptcy before?
7. Are you still employed at (job listed on Statement of Affairs)?
8. Have you filed state and federal tax returns for every year you were required to do so?
9. Do you still maintain the bank accounts listed on your Statement of Affairs?
10. Did you have any other bank accounts on the date of bankruptcy?
11. When was the last one closed?
12. Do you have a safety deposit box?
13. What are its present contents?
14. When was the last time you checked it?
15. Have you sold or transferred anything within the past twelve months?
16. Do you own any real estate?
17. Do you have an interest in the estate of a deceased person?
18. Do you own a car?
19. Are you driving one today?
20. How long has it been since you owned an interest in one?
21. Do you owe any money on it?
22. What is its present condition?
23. What is its present value?
24. Do you own any stock or U.S. Savings Bonds?
25. Have any creditors levied on your earnings?
26. Are there any lawsuits pending in which you are the plaintiff?
27. Do you own anything that isn't listed on the schedules?

Answer each of the questions truthfully. Most of them are the same questions that are on your forms, so be sure to answer them in the same way. When the trustee has finished questioning you, he or she will ask if any of your creditors are present. Remember that each of your creditors got notice of the meeting at the same time you did. You have to be there, but it would be most unusual if any of your creditors bothered to come. If one did, all he or she could do is ask you the same kinds of questions that the trustee did.

The trustee will also give you any notices to creditors that were returned by the post office as undeliverable. If so, you must make sure that the creditor actually knows of your bankruptcy filing. Otherwise, you run the risk that the debt will not be discharged. Check the address on your bills. Double-check the address in the phone book. If your creditor is a person, check with his or her friends or relatives or former employer. Send the creditor copies of your Petition, Statement of Affairs, schedules, and Notice of Meeting of Creditors by registered mail. Keep a copy of the mail receipt for your file.

At the conclusion of the first meeting of creditors, the trustee may give you a business card. If not, ask for one. The trustee is the person in charge of your case. Should you have any questions about the handling of your bankruptcy, you should contact the trustee.

The trustee may wish to contact you, too. This is why, in questioning you, the trustee probably double-checked your job, home address, and phone number. Be sure to let the trustee know if you move before the discharge hearing (see Chapter 10). The successful progress of your case depends on the court and the trustee being able to contact you if necessary. If they can't, you may lose some of your property and your right to discharge a debt.

CHAPTER

10

$$$$$

AFTER THE MEETING

SECURED DEBTS—KEEPING PROPERTY OR GIVING IT BACK

Purchase Money Debts

If you have not already done so, you should decide now whether you wish to keep any exempt property that is security for a debt. Reread Chapter 5, Step 3. I am talking only about secured debts here. You should already know that you can keep property that (1) is not secured by a loan from either the seller or a financial institution that loaned you the money to buy that property, and (2) is also exempt household property under the federal or state exemption system. (See the section in this chapter on nonpurchase money debts.) Now you need only decide whether to surrender or pay for property that you bought with money loaned to you by the creditor to buy that very property.[1] Don't try to keep too much, and don't be influenced by a creditor to keep something that you don't want. You filed bankruptcy to get out of debt— it won't help you very much if you sign up to keep all your old debts. For example, if your secured debts consist of a car, household furniture, jewelry, and a piano, you have to decide whether you want to keep any of these items. If you do not want the property, the debts will be wiped out in bankruptcy, but you will have to turn in the property. If you do want to keep one or more pieces of property, read on.

To keep a piece of property, contact the secured creditor (the person or business to whom you owe the money) and negotiate an amount you must pay and a schedule of repayment. According to law, you must pay either the amount of the debt or the present value of the property, whichever is less. You have already set down your idea of the value of the property in Schedule A-2 (Form 3, page 2). If the secured creditor disagrees with your estimate of value, you have three

choices: (1) you may accept the creditor's estimate of the value of the piece of property and agree to pay that amount in order to keep the property, (2) you may disagree with the creditor's estimate of value and decide to let him or her repossess the property, or (3) you may disagree with the creditor's estimate of value and wish to retain the property. If so, try to make a deal. Remember two things when you negotiate. First, it is never wise to pay more for something than it's worth. If a creditor wants $300 for a $200 chair, let the creditor take it back and go buy one for $200 somewhere else. Second, remember that most of the time the creditor wants to make a deal with you — it's expensive to pick up, recondition, and resell used property. You can probably get to keep some of your property for less than you think if you are a tough bargainer. This is particularly true if you are dealing with a financial institution as opposed to the original seller. A bank or loan company rents money — it doesn't sell property. If at all possible, it doesn't want to have to collect your second-hand goods.

If negotiation does not work, you should contact an attorney to advise you about contesting the creditor's estimate of value. Obviously, it would be wise to see a lawyer only if the difference is considerable. Otherwise you will wind up paying more to the lawyer than the dispute is worth.

If you and the creditor reach an agreement allowing you to keep one or more pieces of property, you will probably have to sign a new contract providing for either payment in full now or the number and amount of monthly installments. Be sure to take a copy of this agreement with you when you go to court for the postdischarge hearing, which we will discuss later in this chapter.

If you do not wish to keep the property, simply call or write the secured creditor and tell him or her to repossess the item. The secured creditor is responsible for picking it up.

A couple of examples may help you to understand the mechanics of keeping or returning secured property.

Louie owns a 1977 Toyota that is the subject of a secured debt. The Blue Book puts the value of the Toyota at $2,400-$2,800. Louie listed the value of the Toyota on Schedule A-2 at $2,100 because it has some body damage. The amount of unpaid debt is $3,200. Louie needs the car to get to work.

After filing for bankruptcy, Louie contacted the secured creditor. He offered to pay the creditor $100 a month for twenty-one months plus interest. The creditor asked for $2,800 now. After some discussion, they reached a compromise. Louie signed a written agreement whereby he agreed to pay the secured creditor $100 a month for twenty-two months plus interest.

Louie knows that, according to law, the secured creditor can insist on payment in full right away. He is willing to pay what he thinks is a little more than the car is worth because the creditor will let him pay over time. And Louie needs the car to get to work. If he can't reach an agreement with the secured creditor, Louie will lose the Toyota, and he doesn't want the hassle of finding another means of transportation. But Louie realizes that it would be silly to pay an unreasonable amount for the car. He has made a budget and has decided that if the creditor isn't reasonable, he will turn the car in and get an old clunker to get to work.

*   *   *

Neil bought an engagement ring for his girlfriend Ginny. At the time of the sale, he signed a written security agreement. The amount of the unpaid debt is $900. Before bankruptcy, Neil took the ring to a jeweler and had it appraised for $1,500. He listed the value of the ring as $1,500 on Schedule A-2 and claimed the ring as exempt property under federal exemption 16.

Neil doesn't really want (or need) the ring anymore because he and Ginny broke up. But he hates to throw a year's worth of payments down the drain. So Neil went in to talk to the secured creditor, the manager of the jewelry store where he bought the ring. Neil offered to pay him $75 a month for twelve months. The manager refused. He wanted $900 in cash or the ring. Since Neil didn't have the money, he decided to sell the ring, and he was successful. A woman who answered his classified ad paid Neil $1,100 in cash for the engagement ring. Neil then paid the jewelry store $900 and put the other $200 in the bank.

Nonpurchase Money Debts

If you have any exempt household goods secured by debts to a creditor who did not sell you the property or loan you the money to buy it, you are free to keep that property after bankruptcy.[2] If you have any doubts about this, reread Chapter 5, Step 3. Remember, though, that in some courts this does not happen automatically—you must ask the judge to allow you to keep the property. If you have any of these kinds of debts, call the bankruptcy clerk and ask if you need to file any papers in order to keep exempt household property secured by a nonpurchase money debt. If you do, here are the papers you must file and instructions on how to prepare them.

1. If you have not already done so, get a copy of any documents you signed from the creditor. You have a right to them.

2. On blank sheets of white paper the same size as the forms, type one copy each of Forms 7-10. Complete the blanks according to the instructions printed on each form. When you have completed the typing, make two copies of each form and the loan papers you got from the creditor. Sign your typewritten copy of Form 7 and staple a copy of the loan papers to each copy of Form 7.

3. Take your three copies of Form 7 (with the loan papers attached) and Form 8 to the bankruptcy clerk with whom you filed Forms 1-5. The clerk will complete the missing blanks on Form 7 and Form 8 and return two copies of each to you.

4. As soon as you leave the clerk's office, address an envelope to the president of the creditor. Put one copy each of Form 7 (with loan papers attached) and Form 8 into the envelope, and seal it. Have a friend put a stamp on the envelope and deposit it in the mailbox. Then take your friend to a notary public. You can find one in the yellow pages. Have your friend sign a copy of Form 9 in the presence of the notary.

5. Take the signed, notarized copy of Form 9 and the other two copies of it to the bankruptcy clerk. Ask the clerk to file it.

6. Wait until the day the clerk filled in on Form 8. If in the meantime you receive papers in opposition to your motion in the mail from the creditor, you must immediately contact an attorney. If the creditor does not mail an Answer to you, you must go to court on the day and time indicated on Form 8. Take along your three copies each of Form 10. When your name is called, step to the front of the room and hand the clerk the three copies of Form 10. The judge will ask you a question or two about the loan and the property you gave as security for the loan. Then the judge will sign a copy of Form 10 and give you back the two copies of it.

7. As soon as you leave the courtroom, address an envelope to the creditor. Put one copy of Form 10 in the envelope, and seal it. Have a friend mail it to the creditor by registered mail.

8. **Breathe a sigh of relief. You have just acted on your own to protect all of your exempt property.**

FORM 7

Your Name
Address
Phone Number
In Propia Persona

UNITED STATES BANKRUPTCY COURT
_____ DISTRICT OF _____

(See instruction 1,   *(Fill in the name*
Form 1.)   *of your state.)*

)
)
IN RE:)
_____, Debtor)
(Fill in your name.)   )
)
)
)   No. _____*(Fill in the*
)   *number the clerk put on*
)   *first page of your forms.)*
_____)

114

MOTION TO AVOID LIEN

(Type in your name),   debtor herein, hereby moves the court for an order under 11 U.S.C. section 522 (f) avoiding a nonpossessory, nonpurchase money security interest in personal and household goods and in support of this motion shows:

1. On or about *(Fill in the date of the loan),* 19___ debtor borrowed *(Fill in the amount of the original debt)* from *(Fill in the name of the creditor).* As security for such debt *(Fill in the name of the creditor)* insisted upon, and debtor executed, a waiver of exemption of certain property, and a security agreement granting to *(Fill in the name of the creditor)* a security interest in and to debtor's personal and household goods. A copy of the security agreement is attached hereto.

2. The money so borrowed from *(Fill in the name of the creditor)* does not represent any part of the purchase price of any of the articles covered in the security agreement which debtor executed, and all of the articles so covered remain in the possession of the debtor and his family.

3. The existence of *(Fill in the name of the creditor)*'s lien on debtor's personal and household goods impairs exemptions to which the debtor would be entitled under *(Type in either "state" or "federal" depending on which exemption system you are claiming)* law.

4. WHEREFORE debtor prays that the court issue an order cancelling and avoiding the security interest of *(Fill in the name of the creditor)* in debtor's personal and household goods.

Dated: _____   _____
      (Fill in date)   *(You sign here)*

FORM 8

UNITED STATES BANKRUPTCY COURT
_____ DISTRICT OF _____

(See instruction 1,   *(Fill in the name*
Form 1.)   *of your state.)*

)
)
IN RE:)
_____, Debtor)
(Fill in your name.))
)
)
) No. _____*(Fill in the*
) *number the clerk put on*
) *first page of your forms.)*
_____)

NOTICE OF MOTION

Please take notice that the attached motion is set for a hearing on *(Leave blank)*, 19 , at o'clock .m., at *(Leave blank)*.

Dated: *(Leave blank)*_____   *(Leave blank)*_____

FORM 9

Your Name
Address
Phone Number
In Propria Persona

UNITED STATES BANKRUPTCY COURT
_____ DISTRICT OF _____

(See instruction 1,   *(Fill in the name*
Form 1.)   *of your state.)*

```
                              )
                              )
        IN RE:                )
        _____, Debtor )
        (Fill in your name.)  )
                              )
                              )
                              )   No. _____(Fill in the
                              )   number the clerk put on
                              )   first page of your forms.)
_____  )
```

AFFIDAVIT OF SERVICE OF PROCESS

1. *(Fill in your friend's name)*, being duly sworn, says that: I am a citizen of the United States. I am over the age of eighteen years and not a party to the within cause.

2. I served the MOTION TO AVOID LIEN and NOTICE OF MOTION on *(Fill in the creditor's name)* on *(Fill in the date of mailing)*, by placing true and correct copies thereof enclosed in a sealed envelope with postage thereon fully prepaid, in the United States post office mail box at *(Fill in the place of mailing)* addressed as follows:

(Fill in the name and address of the creditor)

_____

_____

_____

_____

                              (Your friend signs here)

Subscribed and sworn to before me on *(Leave blank)*, 19__.

_____

                 Notary Public

FORM 10

Your Name
Address
Phone Number
In Propia Persona

UNITED STATES BANKRUPTCY COURT
_____ DISTRICT OF _____

(See instruction 1,   *(Fill in the name*
Form 1.)   *of your state.)*

```
                        )
                        )
IN RE:                  )
_____, Debtor )
(Fill in your name.)    )
                        )
                        )
                        )   No. _____(Fill in the
                        )   number the clerk put on
                        )   first page of your forms.)
_____)
```

ORDER AVOIDING LIEN

It appearing to the court that the lien of *(Fill in the name of the creditor)* is a nonpossessory, nonpurchase money security interest in debtor's household furnishings, appliances, books, musical instruments or jewelry that are held primarily for the personal, family or household use of debtor and his dependents, and that the lien of *(Fill in the name of the creditor)* impairs an exemption to which debtor would have been entitled under law,

Now, therefore, upon the motion of debtor for an order avoiding a nonpossessory, nonpurchase money security interest in personal and household goods, and after a hearing before the court on said motion,

IT IS ORDERED that the nonpossessory, nonpurchase money security interest of *(Fill in creditor's name)* in debtor's personal and household goods be, and it hereby is, cancelled.

Dated: *(Leave blank)*_____   *(Leave blank)*

_____
U.S. Bankruptcy Judge

DEBTS YOU FORGOT TO LIST

Even if you were very careful in preparing your worksheets and bank-ruptcy forms, it may turn out that you have forgotten to list some of your debts. You will not be discharged from having to pay any debt that is not listed somewhere on Schedule A (Form 3). Therefore, as soon as you discover your mistake, you should immediately file an amendment to your forms as well as an amended Creditor List (Form 5).

On a blank piece of paper, type an amendment to Schedule A. It should look like Form 11.

FORM 11

Your Name
Address
Phone Number
In Propia Persona

UNITED STATES BANKRUPTCY COURT
_____ DISTRICT OF _____

(See instruction 1,   *(Type in the name*
Form 1.)   *of your state.)*

)
)

IN RE:)   BANKRUPTCY NO.
)
)

(See instruction 2, Form 1.))   *(Type in the number*
)   *the clerk put on the first*
)   *page of your forms.)*

              Debtor)
_____)

AMENDMENT TO SCHEDULE A   *(Type in the number of the schedule where the debt should have been listed.)*

Petitioner heretofore filed in this court a bankruptcy petition and the schedules as required by law. In the preparation of said schedule the following information was erroneously omitted.

(Type in the name and address of the creditor, the amount and purpose of the debt, and the date the debt was incurred.)

Wherefore, your petitioner hereby amends the schedules heretofore filed in the manner hereinabove set forth.

                                    (You sign here.)
                                 _____
                                 Debtor

State of _____)

County of _____) ss

    I swear under penalty of perjury that I have read the foregoing Amendment to Schedule A and the information contained therein is true and correct to the best of my knowledge, information, and belief.

(You sign here.)
_____

Debtor

Subscribed and sworn to before me on _____ , 19___

    Prepare an Amended Creditor List by retyping Form 5 with the omitted creditor listed in proper alphabetical order.

    File the Amendment to Schedule A and the Amended Creditor List in the same place you filed the original forms. There is an additional filing fee of $10. Mail a copy of all your papers (your Petition, Statement of Affairs, schedules, Amendment to Schedule A, and Notice of Meeting of Creditors) to the creditor for the omitted debt by registered mail.

WHAT IF THE TRUSTEE CONTESTS YOUR LIST OF EXEMPT PROPERTY?

Although it is unlikely that he or she will do so, the trustee has the right to dispute your claims of exempt property listed on Schedule B-4 (Form 4, page 3). If the trustee does, you will receive in the mail a document entitled Objection to Debtor's Claim of Exempt Property. It will identify the particular piece of property that the trustee thinks you should lose by filing bankruptcy. You should immediately consult an attorney about this—unless, of course, the item of property isn't worth enough to justify a lawyer's fees. Remember, you can always represent yourself. Just show up at the designated time and tell the judge why you think your piece of property is on the "exempt" list.

WHAT IF A CREDITOR OPPOSES THE DISCHARGE OF A DEBT?

Again, although it unlikely that they will do so, your creditors have the right to dispute the discharge of a particular debt or even all of your debts.[3] The last date anyone can contest your right to discharge is listed on the notice of the meeting with the trustee. If a creditor wishes to contest the discharge of a debt, he or she will most likely claim that (1) you incurred the debt by use of a false financial statement (see Chapter 5, Step 2), or (2) you incurred the debt by fraud—for example, you deliberately wrote a bad check, went on a shopping spree, or borrowed money after you had already decided on bankruptcy (see Chapter 5, Step 2).

If a creditor wishes to dispute your discharge altogether, he or she will probably say that you have attempted to hide some of your property—perhaps by giving it to friends to keep for you (see Chapter 5, Step 2).

In order to dispute your discharge, the creditor must file a Complaint to Deny Discharge and Determine Debt to Be Nondischargeable. If you should receive a copy of such a document in the mail, you should immediately consult an attorney. In certain instances, if you win and the debt is discharged, your lawyer's fee will be paid by your creditor.

YOUR POSTDISCHARGE HEARING

If all goes well, you will not hear another word about your bankruptcy until two or three months after the meeting with the trustee. At that time, you will receive a notice in the mail setting a date and time for the hearing at which you will be told that you have received your formal discharge from debt. You must attend this hearing. Sometimes the notice of the discharge hearing is at the end of the notice of the meeting of creditors—as with Oscar's. Check yours.

The meeting will be held at the U.S. courthouse where you filed your papers and attended the meeting with the trustee. If neither the trustee nor any of your creditors has filed papers in the meantime, your discharge will have been granted automatically.

Unless you have any of the special problems we just discussed, the hearing will be the first and only time you appear before the bankruptcy judge. Again, you may have to wait your turn, so be prepared to spend an hour or two in court. When your name is called, step forward. The judge will tell you that your discharge has been granted and will ask you whether you wish to "reaffirm" (pay) any of your debts. If you have signed a written agreement to pay one of your secured creditors as discussed earlier in this chapter, give the clerk a copy of that agreement. That debt—and your nondischargeable debts such as taxes and child support (see Chapter 5)—are the only debts you must continue to pay. A creditor cannot enforce any other debt against you.

THE END

Congratulations! It's all over. Good luck on your fresh start—you've earned it. But remember Gloria's closing words:

> My lawyer told me that a lot of his customers go through bankruptcy over and over again all through their lives. I vowed that I'd be different—if I ever get out of this, I'll never do it again. Now I have to live on a real close budget, and I use credit only when there is no alternative. If I get extravagant or forget what I'm doing, I'll blow it. But I'm a survivor. I'm going to make it.

NOTES

1. If you no longer have the property, you don't have a choice. You must repay the debt.
2. If you pledged your car as collateral for a loan, it doesn't matter whether the debt is connected with your purchase of the car. In order to keep it you must pay either the fair market value of the car or the amount of the debt, whichever is less.
3. Some debts are automatically nondischargeable—the creditor doesn't have to do anything. These include family support obligations, student loans, taxes, fines in criminal cases, and debts you forgot to list on Schedule A (Form 3). See Chapter 5, Step 2.

CHAPTER

11

$$$$$

A BANKRUPTCY CHECKLIST

Prepare a list of all your debts. Determine which are dischargeable in bankruptcy and which are not.

Prepare a list of your property. Determine which is exempt under both state and federal law and decide which system is better for you.

Decide whether to file for bankruptcy. Prepare an after-bankruptcy budget and consider your alternatives. Then, if you decide to file for bankruptcy, take the following steps.

1. Stop all credit and credit card purchases. Close your checking account. (Be sure to wait for the last checks to clear.)
2. Convert all nonexempt assets, except the filing fee, into exempt form.
3. Complete the following forms:
   Form 1: Petition for Voluntary Bankruptcy
   Form 2: Statement of Affairs for Debtor Not Engaged in Business
   Form 3: Schedule A (Statement of All Debts of Debtor)
   Form 4: Schedule B (Statement of All Property of Debtor)
   Form 5: Creditor List
4. Sign the Petition, schedules, and Statement of Affairs.
5. Make four copies of each form.
6. File the original and three copies of each form with the clerk of the bankruptcy court in your area, paying a $60 filing fee in cash or by money order.
7. Stop paying all unsecured dischargeable debts. Decide whether you wish to keep any exempt property that is collateral for purchase money-secured debts. If you do, negotiate a plan of repayment with the secured creditor for either the amount of the debt or the present value of the property, whichever is less. If you do not pay this amount, the secured creditor is free to repossess the property.
8. If you have any nonpurchase money debts secured by household

goods, prepare and file your Motion to Avoid Lien. Mail the creditor a copy of your motion and the Notice of Motion. File your Affidavit of Service of Process. If you receive in the mail from the creditor papers in opposition to your motion, contact an attorney immediately. Otherwise, go to the hearing and take the Order you prepared with you. The judge will sign the Order, allowing you to keep your exempt property that is the subject of the non-purchase money security interest. Have a friend mail a copy of the Order to the creditor by registered mail.

9. Wait about three to five weeks after your bankruptcy filing. You will receive in the mail a Notice of First Meeting of Creditors. You must attend this meeting. Take along with you copies of the forms and your checkbook, bankbooks, and tax returns. Be prepared to answer questions about your employment, your debts, and your property.

10. Notify the trustee of any change in your mailing address. This is important because in the next few months, you may receive in the mail (1) an Objection to Debtor's Claim of Exempt Property, indicating that the trustee disputes your claims of exemption, or (2) a Complaint to Deny Discharge and Determine Debt to Be Nondischargeable, indicating that one of your creditors contests your right to discharge his or her debt. If you receive either of these papers in the mail, consult an attorney immediately.

11. Within six months of the date you filed for bankruptcy, you will receive in the mail a Notice of Hearing on Discharge. You must attend this hearing. Unless you volunteer at this time to pay any of your debts — and the judge agrees to let you do so — they are discharged forever. Any later agreement you may make to repay any of those debts is not enforceable against you.

CHAPTER
12

$$$$$

SOME DEFINITIONS

The law of bankruptcy has a language all its own. Here is a list of the key terms and their meanings. Each is also defined and illustrated elsewhere in the book.

Bankruptcy—a procedure whereby a debtor is able to free himself or herself of debt.

Chapter 13—a procedure whereby a debtor is freed of creditor harassment and allowed to keep all of his or her property while attempting to pay his or her debts—in whole or in part—over a three-year period.

Cosigner—a person who guarantees the repayment of a debt; although the debtor's obligation is dischargeable in bankruptcy, the cosigner's is not (unless, of course, the cosigner also declares bankruptcy).

Creditor—the person to whom money is owed.

Debt—a legal obligation to pay money.

Discharge—the formal forgiveness of debt granted by the bankruptcy judge several months after the bankruptcy filing.

Dischargeable debt—an obligation that is forgiven in bankruptcy.

Equity—the value of the property less any debts owed on the property.

Exempt property—the property a debtor is allowed to keep after bankruptcy.

File—to take four copies of the filled-out set of forms and $60 in cash to the bankruptcy clerk and thereby commence bankruptcy proceedings.

Forms—the Petition, Statement of Affairs, Schedule A (Statement of All Liabilities), Schedule B (Statement of All Property), and Creditor List, all of which are filed with the bankruptcy clerk to begin the bankruptcy proceedings.

Homestead—the family residence; a part or even all of the equity in it is exempt property.

Meeting of creditors—a meeting that takes place about a month after the bankruptcy filing at which the trustee asks the debtor questions about his or her property.

Nondischargeable debt — an obligation that cannot be wiped out in bankruptcy.

Nonexempt property — the property a debtor loses in bankruptcy.

Nonpurchase money-secured loan — a debt owed to a creditor who took property that you already owned as security for the repayment of the debt.

Property — all of a debtor's possessions, including the right to receive money from someone in the future.

Purchase money-secured loan — a secured debt owed to the seller or financial institution that loaned you the money to buy the property.

Secured debt — a debt arising from a written security agreement by which the debtor pledges certain property to the repayment of the debt; sometimes it is necessary to pay off all or a portion of the debt in order to retain that property (even though it is exempt) after bankruptcy.

Trustee — the person in charge of a bankruptcy; the trustee's duty is to gather and sell the debtor's nonexempt property and divide the sales proceeds among creditors.

Unsecured debt — any debt that is not secured.

Value — the present worth of property, given its age and present condition.

APPENDIX

STATE EXEMPTION STATUTES

Every effort has been made to make this appendix an accurate listing of state exemption statutes. Your state legislature may, however, have amended them in the meantime (particularly to update dollar exemption amounts, due to the ravages of inflation). Therefore, to be on the safe side, you should double-check your state's exemption laws, either by yourself in a law library or by a brief consultation with an attorney.

NOTE: The following states do not allow use of the federal exemption systems: Alabama, Alaska, Arizona, Arkansas, Colorado, Delaware, Florida, Georgia, Idaho, Illinois, Indiana, Iowa, Kansas, Kentucky, Louisiana, Maine, Maryland, Missouri, Montana, Nebraska, Nevada, New Hampshire, New York, North Carolina, North Dakota, Ohio, Oklahoma, Oregon, South Carolina, South Dakota, Tennessee, Utah, Virginia, West Virginia, Wyoming.

ALABAMA

HOMESTEAD
Limitation of value: $5,000
Limitation of area: 160 acres (Alabama Code Title 6 § 10-2)
   NOTE: If a debtor does not claim the homestead exemption, he or she may claim up to a value of $5,000 in a mobile home or similar dwelling if the principal place of residence of the individual   (Ala. Code Title 6 § 10-2)

WAGES
75% of earned but unpaid wages (Ala. Code Title 6 § 10-7)

PERSONAL PROPERTY
Personal property to a value of $3,000 (Alabama Constitution, Article X, § 204 and Ala. Code Title 6 § 10-6)
All necessary and proper wearing apparel, family portraits or pictures, books (Ala. Code Title 6 § 10-6)
A burial place and church pew (Ala. Code Title 6 § 10-5)

INSURANCE
A life insurance policy if the beneficiaries are the debtor's spouse and/or children (Ala. Code Title 6 § 10-8)

PENSIONS
Those received from the state employee's retirement system (Ala. Code Title 36 § 27-28) or teachers' retirement system (Ala. Code Title 16 § 25-23)

PUBLIC BENEFITS
Public assistance (Ala. Code Title 38 § 4-8)
Workmen's compensation (Ala. Code Title 25 § 5-86(b))
Unemployment insurance (Ala. Code Title 25 § 4-140)

STATE EXEMPTION STATUTES

ALASKA

HOMESTEAD
Limitation of value: $27,000 (Alaska Statutes §9.38.010)

WAGES
Weekly net earnings to a value of $175 (Alaska Statutes §9.38.030)

TOOLS OF TRADE
Implements, professional books, and tools of trade to a value of $1400 (Alaska Statutes §9.38.020)

PERSONAL PROPERTY
Burial plot (Alaska Stat. §9.38.015)
Household goods, wearing apparel, books, musical instruments, family portraits and heir-looms, jewelry to a value of $500, pets to a value of $500, a motor vehicle to a value of $1,500 (if the full value of the motor vehicle does not exceed $10,000) (Alaska Stat. §9.38.020)
NOTE: The aggregate value of personal property and tools of trade may not exceed $1,500.

INSURANCE
Medical benefits (Alaska Statutes §9.38.015)
Life Insurance and annuity contracts to a loan value of $5,000 (Alaska Statutes §9.38.025)

PENSIONS
Those received from the teachers or public employees' retirement system (Alaska Stat. §9.38.015)

PUBLIC BENEFITS
Public assistance (Alaska Stat. § 47.25.210)
Old-age assistance (Alaska Stat. § 47.25.550)
Disability (Alaska Stat. § 47.25.880)
Workers' compensation (Alaska Stat. §23.30.160
Unemployment insurance (Alaska Stat. §23.20.405)
Crime victims' reparations (Alaska Stat. §9.38.015)

ARIZONA

HOMESTEAD
Limitation of value: $50,000 (Arizona Revised Statutes §33-1101)

WAGES
A minimum of 75% of earned but unpaid wages (for low-income debtors, the exemption may be higher under a formula based on a multiple of the federal minimum wage) (Ariz. Rev. Stat. §33-1131)

TOOLS OF TRADE
Tools, equipment, instruments and books used in commercial activity, trade, business, or a profession to a total value of $2,500.
Farm machinery, utensils, instruments of husbandry, feed, seed, grain and animals to a total value of $2,500. (Ariz. Rev. Stat. §33-1130)

PERSONAL PROPERTY
The following property to a value of $4,000: a kitchen table and dining room table with four chairs each (plus an additional chair for each additional family member), a living room couch, a living room chair for each family member, three living room coffee or end tables, three living room lamps, one living room carpet or rug, two beds (plus an additional bed for each additional family member), one bed table, dresser and lamp for each bed, bedding, pictures, oil paintings and drawings drawn or painted by the debtor, family portraits, one television set or one radio or stereo, radio alarm clock, one stove, one refrigerator, one washing machine, one clothes dryer, and one vacuum cleaner (Ariz. Rev. Stat. §33-1123)
Food, fuel, and provisions for six months (Ariz. Rev. Stat. §33-1124)
Wearing apparel to a value of $500
Musical instruments to a total value of $250

133

Domestic pets, horses, milk cows, and poultry to a total value of $500
Engagement and wedding rings to a total of $1,000
A motor vehicle to a value of $1,500
Books to a total value of $250
One watch to a value of $100
One typewriter, one bicycle, one sewing machine, the family bible, a burial plot, one
   shotgun, and one rifle to a total value of $500 (Ariz. Rev. Stat. §33-1125)
Life insurance proceeds to a value of $20,000
Prepaid rent (including security deposits) for one and one-half months to a value of
   $1,000
$100 on deposit in a financial institution if an election is filed at the branch office
   (Ariz. Rev. Stat. §33-1126)

INSURANCE
The cash surrender value of life insurance policies if the beneficiaries are family
   members, to a value of $1,000 per beneficiary, not to exceed a total value of $5,000
Health, accident, and disability insurance benefits
Insurance claims for damage to exempt property (Ariz. Rev. Stat. §33-1126)

PENSIONS
Those received from the rangers' pension fund (Ariz. Rev. Stat. §41-955), the state
   employees' retirement system, or municipal pension plans (Ariz. Rev. Stat. §38-762)
75% of all other pension benefits (Ariz. Rev. Stat. §33-1131)

PUBLIC BENEFITS
Welfare benefits (Ariz. Rev. Stat. §46-208)
Workers' compensation (Ariz. Rev. Stat. §23-1068)
Unemployment insurance (Ariz. Rev. Stat. §23-783)

ARKANSAS

HOMESTEAD
A head of a family may claim real property as a homestead. If limited to less than ¼ acre
   in a city, town, or village, or 80 acres elsewhere, there is no value limitation. If
   between ¼ acre and 1 acre in a city, town, or village, or between 80 and 160 acres elsewhere, a $2,500 limitation in value applies. No homestead may exceed 1 acre in a city,
   town, or village, or 160 acres elsewhere. (Arkansas Constitution Article 9 §§ 3-5)
Alternatively, a debtor may claim real or personal property used as a residence to a value
   of $800 if the debtor is unmarried, or $1250 if the debtor is married (Arkansas Statutes
   § 36-211)

WAGES
Earned but unpaid wages if, together with personal property, they do not exceed the $500/
   $200 value limit mentioned below---but in no event less than $25 a week (Ark. Stat. § 30-207)

TOOLS OF TRADE
Implements, professional books or tools to a value of $750 (Ark. Stat. § 36-211)

PERSONAL PROPERTY
A motor vehicle to a value of $1200
Wedding bands including diamonds not exceeding one-half carat in weight (Ark. Stat. § 36-211)
Any personal property of one's choice to a total value of $500 (if married or the head of a
   family) or $200 (if single), and the wearing apparel of the debtor and/or family (Ark.
   Const. Art. 9 §§ 1,2)

INSURANCE
All monies paid or payable from life, health, accident, and disability policies (Ark. Stat.
   § 30-208)

PENSIONS
Those received from state teachers' retirement fund (Ark. Stat. § 80-1443.9-9.14) and state
   police pensions (Ark. Stat. § 42-458)

PUBLIC BENEFITS
Welfare or public assistance benefits (Ark. Stat. §83-133)
Workers' compensation (Ark. Stat. §81-1321)
Unemployment insurance (Ark. Stat. §81-1118)

CALIFORNIA

HOMESTEAD
A member of a family unit or a person over the age of 65 may claim a house, a mobile home,
   boat, or condominium in which he/she actually resides to a value of $45,000. Other debtors
   may claim such property to a value of $30,000. (California Code of Civil Procedure §704.730).

WAGES

75% of earnings paid within the preceding 30 days, 100% if your earnings were subject to an earnings withholding order or wage assignment for support (Calif. C.C.P. 704.070).

A minimum of 75% of earned but unpaid wages (for low-income debtors, the exemption may be higher under a formula based on a multiple of the federal minimum wage)(Calif. C.C.P. §706.050).

Public employee's vacation credits (Calif. C.C.P. §704.113).

TOOLS OF TRADE

Tools, implements, instruments, materials, uniforms, furnishings, books, equipment, one motor vehicle (if no other is exempted which is reasonably adequate for use in the debtor's trade, business or profession) and other personal property reasonably necessary to and actually used by the debtor to earn a livelihood to a value of $2500. (Calif. C.C.P. §704.060).

PERSONAL PROPERTY

One or more motor vehicles to an aggregate value of $1200 (Calif. C.C.P. §704.010).

Household furnishings, appliances, provisions, wearing apparel and other personal effects ordinarily and reasonably necessary to and personally used by the debtor.

NOTE: The court may consider whether the particular item is ordinarily found in a household and whether the item has extraordinary value as compared to the value of items of the same type found in other households. (Calif. C.C.P. §704.020).

Material about to be applied to the repair or improvement of debtor's principal place of residence to a value of $1000 (Calif. C.C.P. 704.030).

Jewelry, heirlooms, and works of art to an aggregate value of $2500 (Calif. C.C.P. §704.040).

Health aids (Calif. C.C.P. §704.050)

$500 on deposit in an account in which payments authorized by the Social Security Administration are directly deposited (Calif. C.C.P. §704.080)

Funds in an inmate's trust account to a value of $1000 (Calif. C.C.P. §704.090)

Personal injury causes of action and recoveries to the extent necessary to support the debtor and his/her family, or, if paid in installments, then a minimum of 75% (Calif. C.C.P. §704.140)

Wrongful death causes of action and recoveries to the extent necessary to support the debtor and his/her family, or, if paid in installments, then a minimum of 75% (Cal. C.C.P. 704.150)

Family burial plot (Calif. C.C.P. §704.200)

Cash or bank accounts to the extent they can be traced to an exempt asset (e.g., earnings paid during previous 30 days, unemployment, disability, or workers' compensation, pension or public assistance benefits, etc.) (Calif. C.C.P. §703.080)

INSURANCE

Life insurance policies to an aggregate loan value of $4000 (Calif. C.C.P. §704.100)

Disability and health insurance benefits (Calif. C.C.P. §704.130)

PENSIONS

Public retirement system funds and benefits (Calif. C.C.P. §704.110) and private retirement plans (including IRAS and Keoghs) to the extent necessary to support the debtor and his/her family at retirement (Calif. C.C.P. §704.115)

PUBLIC BENEFITS

Unemployment benefits and benefits payable by a union due to a labor dispute (Calif. C.C.P. §704.120)

Workers compensation (Calif. C.C.P. §704.160)

Public assistance (Calif. C.C.P. §704.170)

Relocation benefits (Calif. C.C.P. §704.180)

Financial aid to students (Calif. C.C.P. §704.190)

COLORADO

HOMESTEAD

Real property or a mobile home to a value of $20,000 (Colorado Revised Statutes §§38-41-201 and 38-41-201.6)

WAGES

A minimum of 75% of earned but unpaid wages (for low-income debtors, the exemption may be higher under a formula based on a multiple of the federal minimum wage) (Col. Rev. Stat. § 13-54-104)

TOOLS OF TRADE

Stock in trade, supplies, fixtures, maps, machines, tools, equipment, books, and business materials to a value of $1500

Library of a professional person to a value of $1500

Livestock and poultry to a value of $3000 and horses, mules, wagons, carts, machinery, harness, implements and tools to a value of $2000 (Col. Rev. Stat. § 13-54-102)

PERSONAL PROPERTY
Wearing apparel to a value of $750
Watches, jewelry and articles of adornment to a value of $500
Library, family pictures, and school books to a value of $750
One burial plot per family member
Household goods to a value of $1500
Provisions and fuel to a value of $300
Motor vehicles used to carry on a gainful occupation to a value of $1000
Personal injury recoveries (Col. Rev. Stat. § 13-54-102)

INSURANCE
Insurance claims for damage to exempt property (Col. Rev. Stat. § 13-54-102)
Avails of life insurance policies to a value of $5000 (Col. Rev. Stat. § 13-54-102)
Group life insurance (Col. Rev. Stat. § 10-7-205)
Disability insurance benefits --- periodic payments of up to $200 per month (Col. Rev.
    Stat. § 10-8-114)

PENSIONS
Those received from teachers' retirement fund (Col. Rev. Stat. § 22-64-120)
State retirement fund (Col. Rev. Stat. § 24-51-120)
Public employees' retirement fund (Col. Rev. Stat. § 24-51-219)
Police pension fund (Col. Rev. Stat. § 31-30-313)
Firemen's pension fund (Col. Rev. Stat. § 31-30-412 and § 31-30-518)
Military pensions for service in time of war or armed conflict (Col. Rev. Stat. § 13-54-102)
75% of all other pension benefits (Col. Rev. Stat. § 13-54-104)

PUBLIC BENEFITS
Public assistance (Col. Rev. Stat. § 26-2-131)
Workmen's compensation (Col. Rev. Stat. § 8-52-107)
Unemployment insurance (Col. Rev. Stat. § 8-80-103)
Crime victim reparations (Col. Rev. Stat. § 13-54-102)

CONNECTICUT

WAGES
A minimum of 75% of earned but unpaid wages (for low-income debtors, the exemption may be
    higher under a formula based on a multiple of the federal minimum wage) (Connecticut
    General Statutes Annotated § 52-361)

TOOLS OF TRADE
Tools, books, instruments, and farm animals necessary to the debtor in the course of his
    or her occupation or profession
Arms and military equipment, uniforms, and musical instruments owned by any member of the
    militia or U.S. armed forces (Conn. Gen. Stat. Ann. § 52-352b)

PERSONAL PROPERTY
Necessary apparel, bedding, foodstuffs, household furniture, and appliances
Burial plot (Conn. Gen. Stat. Ann. § 52-352b)
A motor vehicle to a value of $1,500
Wedding and engagement rings
Residential utility deposits and security deposits (Conn. Gen. Stat. Ann. § 52-352c)

INSURANCE
Health and disability insurance benefits (Conn. Gen. Stat. Ann. § 52-352b)

PENSIONS
Those received from the state employees' retirement system (Conn. Gen. Stat. Ann. § 5-171)
    and the municipal employees' retirement fund (Conn. Gen. Stat. Ann. § 7-446)
75% of all other pension benefits (Conn. Gen. Stat. Ann. § 52-352c)

PUBLIC BENEFITS
Public assistance payments and any wages earned by the recipient under an incentive earnings
    or similar program
Workers' compensation
Social Security
Veterans' benefits
Unemployment insurance (Conn. Gen. Stat. Ann. § 52-352b)
Awards for crime reparations (Conn. Gen. Stat. Ann. § 52-352c)

DELAWARE

WAGES
85% of earned but unpaid wages (Delaware Code Annotated Title 10 § 4913)

TOOLS OF TRADE .
Tools, implements, and fixtures necessary for carrying on the debtor's trade or business,
    to a value of $75 for residents of New Castle and Sussex Counties, and to $50 for
    residents of Kent County (Del. Code Ann. Tit. 10 § 4902)

PERSONAL PROPERTY
All debtors may exempt:
Family Bible, school books, family library, family pictures, a church pew, a burial plot, a sewing machine and wearing apparel (Del. Code Ann. Tit. 10 § 4902)
In addition, a head of family who resides in New Castle County may exempt other personal property to a value of $200; and a head of family who resides in Kent County may exempt additional household goods to a value of $150 (Del. Code Ann. Tit. 10 § 4903)

INSURANCE
A life insurance policy (Del. Code Ann. Tit. 18 § 2725)
Health and disability insurance benefits (Del. Code Ann. Tit. 18 § 2726)
Group life insurance (Del. Code Ann. Tit. 18 § 2727)
Annuities --- periodic payments of up to $350 per month (Del. Code Ann. Tit. 18 § 2728)

PENSIONS
Those received from Sussex County employees' pension fund (Del. Code Ann. Tit. 9 § 6415) and Kent County employees' pension fund (Del. Code Ann. Tit. 9 § 4316)

PUBLIC BENEFITS
Workmen's compensation (Del. Code Ann. Tit. 19 § 2355)
Unemployment insurance (Del. Code Ann. Tit. 19 § 3374)

DISTRICT OF COLUMBIA

WAGES
A debtor who is the principal support of his or her family may exempt a maximum of $200 per month of earned but unpaid wages. Other debtors may exempt $60 per month of earned but unpaid wages (District of Columbia Code § 15-503)

TOOLS OF TRADE
Mechanic's tools to a value of $200
Stock and materials for carrying on a business to a value of $200
Library, office furniture, and implements of a professional person or artist to a value of $300 (D.C. Code § 15-501)

PERSONAL PROPERTY
Wearing apparel to a value of $300
Beds, bedding, household furniture and furnishings, sewing machine, radio, stove, and cooking utensils to a value of $300
One horse or mule; one cart, wagon, or dray and harness, or one motor vehicle to a value of $500 if used principally by the debtor in his or her trade or business
Fuel and provisions for three montns
Family pictures
Family library to a value of $400 (D.C. Code § 15-501)

INSURANCE
Disability insurance benefits (D.C. Code § 35-522)
Group life insurance (D.C. Code § 35-523)
Avails of life insurance policies (D.C. Code § 35-521)

PENSIONS
Those received from the public school teachers' retirement fund (D.C. Code § 31-1217)
Other pensions in an amount not to exceed $200 per month if the debtor is the principal support of his or her family, $60 per month otherwise (D.C. Code § 15-503)

PUBLIC BENEFITS
Unemployment insurance (D.C. Code § 46-119)

FLORIDA

HOMESTEAD
A head of family may claim property limited in area to ½ acre if within a municipality or 160 acres elsewhere, or a mobile home or modular home (Florida Constitution Article 10 § 4 and Florida Statutes Annotated § 222.05)

WAGES
A head of family may exempt 100% of earned but unpaid wages (Fla. Stat. Ann. § 222.11)

PERSONAL PROPERTY
A head of family may exempt personal property to a value of $1,000 (Fla. Const. Art. 10 § 4)

INSURANCE

Life insurance policies and annuity contracts (Fla. Stat. Ann. § 222.14)
Disability insurance benefits (Fla. Stat. Ann. § 222.18)

Those received from state retirement system (Fla. Stat. Ann. § 121.131), firemen's pension
    fund (Fla. Stat. Ann. § 175.241), police officers' retirement trust fund (Fla. Stat. Ann.
    § 185.25), highway patrol pension fund (Fla. Stat. Ann. § 321.22), teachers' retirement
    system (Fla. Stat. Ann. § 238.15), and state and county officers' and employees' retire-
    ment system (Fla. Stat. Ann. § 122.15)

PUBLIC BENEFITS
Unemployment insurance (Fla. Stat. Ann. § 443.051)
Workers' compensation (Fla. Stat. Ann. § 440.22)

GEORGIA

HOMESTEAD
Limitation of value: $5,000 (Georgia Code Annotated §44-13-100)

TOOLS OF TRADE
Implements, professional books or tools to a value of $500 (Georgia Code Ann. §44-13-100)

PERSONAL PROPERTY
Motor vehicles to a value of $1,000
Household furnishings, household goods, wearing apparel, appliances, books, animals, crops
    and musical instruments to a value of $200 per item, $3,500 in the aggregate
Jewelry to a value of $500
Other property to a value of $400 together with any unused amount of the homestead exemp-
    tion
Wrongful death recoveries and life insurance proceeds (if reasonably necessary to support
    the debtor) and personal injury recoveries to a value of $7,500 (Georgia Code Ann.
    §44-13-100)

INSURANCE
Disability and health insurance benefits
A life insurance policy to a cash surrender value of $2,000 (Georgia Code Ann. §44-13-100)

PENSIONS
100% if reasonably necessary for the support of the debtor and his/her family (Georgia Code
    Ann. §44-13-100)

PUBLIC BENEFITS
Social Security benefits
Unemployment compensation
Public assistance
Veterans' benefits
Crime victim awards (Georgia Code Ann. §44-13-100)

HAWAII

HOMESTEAD
A head of household or an individual aged 65 or older may exempt real property to a value
    of $30,000. Anyone else may exempt real property to a value of $20,000 (Hawaii Revised
    Statutes § 651-92)

WAGES
100% of earned but unpaid wages for services rendered in the past 31 days (Ha. Rev. Stat.
    § 651-121)

TOOLS OF TRADE
Tools of trade including tools, implements, instruments, uniforms, furnishings, books,
    equipment, one commercial fishing boat and nets, and one motor vehicle (Ha. Rev. Stat
    § 651-121)

PERSONAL PROPERTY
Household furnishings and appliances
Books and wearing apparel
Jewelry, watches, and items of personal adornment to a value of $1,000
A motor vehicle to a value of $1,000
A burial plot (Ha. Rev. Stat. § 651-121)

INSURANCE
Insurance claims for damage to exempt property (Ha. Rev. Stat. § 651-121)
Disability insurance benefits (Ha. Rev. Stat. § 431-439)
Life insurance policies if the beneficiaries are the debtor's spouse and/or children (Ha. Rev. Stat. § 431-440)
Group life insurance policies (Ha. Rev. Stat. § 431-440)

PENSIONS
Received from the state or municipal subdivisions (Ha. Rev. Stat. § 653-3)

PUBLIC BENEFITS
Workmen's compensation (Ha. Rev. Stat. § 386-57)
Unemployment insurance (Ha. Rev. Stat. § 383-163)

IDAHO

HOMESTEAD
A head of family may claim real property limited in value to $25,000. Any other person may claim real property limited in value to $12,000 (Idaho Code § 55-1201)

WAGES
75% of earned but unpaid wages (for low-income debtors, the exemption may be higher under a formula based on a multiple of the federal minimum wage) (Idaho Code § 11-207)

TOOLS OF TRADE
Implements, professional books, and tools of trade to a value of $1,000; arms, uniforms, and accoutrements required of a peace officer, member of the national guard, or military (Idaho Code § 11-605)

PERSONAL PROPERTY
A burial plot (Idaho Code §11-603)
Personal injury and wrongful death recoveries (Idaho Code §11-604)
Furnishings and appliances, including one firearm, wearing apparel, animals, books, musical instruments, family portraits, and heirlooms of particular sentimental value to a value per item of $500
Jewelry to a value of $250
A motor vehicle to a value of $500
A water right not to exceed 160 inches of water for irrigation of lands actually cultivated by the debtor
Crops grown or growing on 50 acres of land cultivated by the debtor to a value of $1,000 (Idaho Code §11-605)

INSURANCE
Health insurance benefits (Idaho Code § 11-603)
Disability insurance benefits (Idaho Code § 11-604)
Insurance proceeds for damage to exempt property (Idaho Code § 11-606)
Life insurance policies (Idaho Code § 41-1833)
Group life insurance (Idaho Code § 41-1835)
Annuities --- periodic payments of up to $350 per month (Idaho Code § 41-1836)

PENSIONS
Those received from public employees' retirement system (Idaho Code § 59-1325)
Stock bonus, pension, and profit-sharing plans (Idaho Code § 11-604)

PUBLIC BENEFITS
Social Security, unemployment insurance, veterans' benefits, and public assistance (Idaho Code § 11-603)
Workers' compensation (Idaho Code § 72-802)

ILLINOIS

HOMESTEAD
Limitation of value: $7,500 (Illinois Code of Civil Procedure §12-901)

WAGES
85% of earned but unpaid wages (for low-income debtors, the exemption may be higher under a formula based on a multiple of the federal minimum wage) (Ill. Code of Civ. Proc. §12-803)

TOOLS OF TRADE
Implements, professional books or tools of trade to a value of $750 (Ill. Code of Civ. Proc. §12-1001)

PERSONAL PROPERTY
Necessary wearing apparel, bible, school books and family pictures
Motor vehicle to a value of $1,200
Wrongful death recoveries and life insurance proceeds (if reasonably necessary to support the debtor) and personal injury recoveries to a value of $7,500
Other property to a value of $2,000 (Ill. Code of Civ. Proc. §12-1001)

INSURANCE
Life insurance policies if the beneficiaries are the debtor's spouse and/or dependents (Ill. Code of Civ. Proc. §12-1001)

PENSIONS
All pensions or retirement funds (Ill. Code of Civ. Proc. §12-1001)

PUBLIC BENEFITS
Social security benefits
Unemployment compensation
Public assistance
Veterans benefits
Crime victim reparations (Ill. Code of Civ. Proc. §12-1001)

INDIANA

HOMESTEAD
Real estate or personal property constituting the personal or family residence of the debtor to a value of $7,500 (Indiana Statutes Annotated § 34-2-28-1)

WAGES
75% of earned but unpaid wages (for low-income debtors, the exemption may be higher under a formula based on a multiple of the federal minimum wage) (Ind. Stat. Ann. § 24-4.5-5-105)

PERSONAL PROPERTY
A debtor may exempt other real or tangible personal property to a value of $4,000 and intangible personal property (other than debts owing and income owing) to a value of $100
NOTE: In no event can the total of all exempted property (the homestead, other real property, and personal property) exceed $10,000 (Ind. Stat. Ann. § 34-2-28-1)

INSURANCE
Life insurance policies if the beneficiaries are the debtor's spouse and/or dependents (Ind. Stat. Ann. § 27-1-12-14)
Group life insurance (Ind. Stat. Ann. § 27-1-12-29)

PENSIONS
100% of pensions received from the police pension fund (Ind. Stat. Ann. § 19-1-18-21, 19-1-24-4), firemen's pension fund (Ind. Stat. Ann. § 19-1-36.5-15, 19-1-37-22), municipal utilities pension fund (Ind. Stat. Ann. § 19-3-31-5), and state teachers' retirement fund (Ind. Stat. Ann. § 21-6.1-5-17)

PUBLIC BENEFITS
Supplemental assistance to the blind (Ind. Stat. Ann. § 12-1-6-12) or to the disabled (Ind. Stat. Ann. § 12-1-7.1-14)
Workmen's compensation (Ind. Stat. Ann. § 22-3-2-17)
Unemployment insurance (Ind. Stat. Ann. § 22-4-33-3)

IOWA

HOMESTEAD
A debtor may claim real property as a family homestead limited in area to ½ acre if within a city or town plat and 40 acres elsewhere (Iowa Code Annotated § 561.2)

WAGES
75% of earned but unpaid wages (for low-income debtors, the exemption may be higher under a formula based on a multiple of the federal minimum wage) (Iowa Code Ann. § 642.21)

PERSONAL PROPERTY
Wearing apparel to a value of $200 per item, $1000 in the aggregate
One shotgun and either a rifle or musket
Library, family Bibles, portraits, pictures and paintings to a value of $200 per item, $1000
   in the aggregate
A burial plot
Two cows, two calves, fifty sheep, six stands of bees, poultry to a value of $100, five hogs and
   all pigs under six months of age, and feed for the animals for six months
Household furnishings, household goods, and appliances to a value of $200 per item, $2,000 in
   the aggregate
Any combination of the following to a value of $5000:
   a. musical instruments
   b. a motor vehicle to a value of $1200
   c. proper implements, professional books, or tools of trade
   d. a team, and the wagon or other vehicle with the proper harness or tackle, and other
      necessary implements of husbandry
   e. wages and tax refunds to a value of $1000 (Iowa Code Ann. § 627.6)

INSURANCE
Life insurance (Iowa Code Ann. § 627.6)

PENSIONS
100% of pensions received from the fire or police retirement system (Iowa Code Ann.
   § 410.11 and § 410.13) and the federal government (Iowa Code Ann. § 627.8)
75% of all other pension benefits (Iowa Code Ann. §642.21)

PUBLIC BENEFITS
Social security benefits
Unemployment compensation
Public assistance
Veterans benefits
Disability benefits (Iowa Code Ann. §627.6)
Workers' compensation (Iowa Code Ann. §627.13)
Adopted child assistance (Iowa Code Ann. §627.19)

KANSAS

HOMESTEAD
Limitation of area: 160 acres of farming land or one acre within the limits of an incorporated town or city, or a mobile home (Kansas Statutes Annotated §60-2301)

WAGES
A minimum of 75% of earned but unpaid wages (for low-income debtors, the exemption may be
   higher under a formula based on a multiple of the federal minimum wage) (Ks. Stat. Ann.
   § 60-2310)

TOOLS OF TRADE
Books, documents, furniture, instruments, tools, implements and equipment, breeding stock,
   seed grain or growing plant stock, or other tangible means of production regularly and
   reasonably necessary in carrying on his or her profession, trade, business, or occupation
   to an aggregate value of $5,000 (Ks. Stat. Ann. § 60-2304)

PERSONAL PROPERTY
Furnishings, equipment, and supplies, including food, fuel, and clothing for one year
Ornaments of his or her person, including jewelry to a value of $500
One means of conveyance
Burial plot (Ks. Stat. Ann. §60-2304)

INSURANCE
A life insurance policy (Ks. Stat. Ann. § 40-414)

PENSIONS
Pensions from the U.S. government if necessary for the maintenance or support of the
   family (Ks. Stat. Ann. § 60-2308)
Pensions received from the state school retirement system (Ks. Stat. Ann. § 72-5526),
   police and fire department retirement systems (Ks. Stat. Ann. § 13-14a10) or public
   employees' retirement system (Ks. Stat. Ann. § 74-4923)

PUBLIC BENEFITS
Social welfare payments (Ks. Stat. Ann. § 39-717)
Workmen's compensation (Ks. Stat. Ann. § 44-514)
Unemployment insurance (Ks. Stat. Ann. § 44-718)

KENTUCKY

HOMESTEAD
Limitation of value: $5,000 (Kentucky Revised Statutes § 427.060)

WAGES
A minimum of 75% of earned but unpaid wages (for low-income debtors, the exemption may be higher under a formula based on a multiple of the federal minimum wage) (Ky. Rev. Stat. § 427.010)

TOOLS OF TRADE
Tools, equipment, and livestock, including poultry, of a farmer to a value of $3,000 (Ky. Rev. Stat. § 427.010)
Necessary tools of a mechanic or skilled artisan to a value of $300 (Ky. Rev. Stat. § 427.030)
The professional library, office equipment, instruments, and furnishings of a minister, attorney, physician, surgeon, chiropractor, veterinarian, or dentist to a value of $1,000 (Ky. Rev. Stat. § 427.040)

PERSONAL PROPERTY
All household furnishings, jewelry, personal clothing, and ornaments to a value of $3,000
A motor vehicle to a value of $2,500 (Ky. Rev. Stat. § 427.010)
Other property to a value of $1,000 (Ky. Rev. Stat. § 427.160)
Personal injury recoveries to a value of $7,500 (Ky. Rev. Stat. § 427.150)

INSURANCE
A life insurance policy (Ky. Rev. Stat. § 304.14-300)
Health and disability insurance benefits (Ky. Rev. Stat. § 304.14-310)
Group life insurance (Ky. Rev. Stat. § 304.14-320)
Annuities --- periodic payments of up to $350 per month (Ky. Rev. Stat. § 304.14-330)

PENSIONS
Those received from police and firefighter's pension funds (Ky. Rev. Stat. § 427.120 and § 427.125), retirement systems of teachers (Ky. Rev. Stat. § 161.700), and state employees retirement system (Ky. Rev. Stat. § 61.690)

PUBLIC BENEFITS
Workmen's compensation (Ky. Rev. Stat. § 342.180)
Unemployment insurance (Ky. Rev. Stat. § 341.470)
Public assistance (Ky. Rev. Stat. §205.220)
Awards for crime reparations (Ky. Rev. Stat. §427.150)

LOUISIANA

HOMESTEAD
Limitation of value: $15,000 (Louisiana Revised Statutes § 20:1)

WAGES
A minimum of 75% of earned but unpaid wages (for low-income debtors, the exemption may be higher under a formula based on a multiple of the federal minimum wage) (La. Rev. Stat. § 13:3881)

TOOLS OF TRADE
The tools, instruments, or books necessary to the trade, calling, or profession of the debtor, including one pickup truck with a gross weight of less than three tons, or one non-luxury automobile and one utility trailer (La. Rev. Stat. §13:3881)

PERSONAL PROPERTY
Clothing, bedding linen, chinaware, nonsterling silverware, glassware, livingroom, bedroom, and diningroom furniture, cooking stove, heating and cooling equipment, sewing machine, kitchen utensils, pressing irons, washer, dryer, refrigerator, freezer, family portraits, arms and military accoutrements, musical instruments, poultry, fowl and one cow, income from total property (La. Rev. Stat. §13:3881)

INSURANCE
Proceeds of health and accident and disability insurance policies (La. Rev. Stat. § 22:646)
Proceeds and avails of life insurance policies (La. Rev. Stat. § 22:647)

PENSIONS
All pensions and annuities (La. Rev. Stat. § 20:33)

PUBLIC BENEFITS
Public assistance (La. Rev. Stat. § 46:111)
Workmen's compensation (La. Rev. Stat. § 23:1205)
Unemployment insurance (La. Rev. Stat. § 23:1693)

MAINE

HOMESTEAD
Limitation in value: $7,500 (Maine Revised Statutes Annotated Title 14 § 4422)

TOOLS OF TRADE
Implements, professional books or tools of trade, including power tools, materials and
    stock, to a value of $1,000 (Maine Rev. Stat. Ann. Tit. 14 § 4422)
One of every type of farm implement used to raise and harvest agricultural products
    commercially
One boat, not exceeding 5 tons burden, used for commercial fishing (Maine Rev. Stat. Ann.
    Tit. 14 § 4422)

PERSONAL PROPERTY
A motor vehicle to a value of $1,200
Household furnishings, household goods, wearing apparel, appliances, books, animals, crops
    and musical instruments to a value of $200 per item
A wedding ring and an engagement ring, and other jewelry to a value of $500
One cooking stove, all furnaces or stoves used for heating, 10 cords of wood, 5 tons of
    coal, and 1000 gallons of petroleum products
Food for six months, all seeds, fertilizers, feed and other material to raise and harvest
    food through one growing season, and tools and equipment for raising and harvesting food
Wrongful death recoveries and life insurance proceeds (if reasonably necessary to support
    the debtor) and personal injury recoveries to a value of $7,500
Other property to a value of $400 ($4,900 of additional tools of trade, personal injury
    recoveries and household goods, etc. if the homestead exemption is not claimed) (Maine
    Rev. Stat. Ann. Tit. 14 § 4422)

INSURANCE
A life insurance policy to a cash surrender value of $4,000
Disability and health insurance benefits (Maine Rev. Stat. Ann. Tit. 14 § 4422)

PENSIONS
100% of pensions if reasonably necessary for the support of the debtor (Maine Rev. Stat.
    Ann. Tit. 14 § 4422)

PUBLIC BENEFITS
Social Security, unemployment insurance, public assistance, veterans' benefits and crime
    victim awards (Maine Rev. Stat. Ann. Tit. 14 § 4422)

MARYLAND

WAGES
A minimum of 75% of earned but unpaid wages (for low-income debtors, the exemption may be
    higher, namely $120 per week or a formula based on a multiple of the federal minimum
    wage) (Maryland Annotated Code of Commercial Law § 15-601.1)

TOOLS OF TRADE
Wearing apparel, books, tools, instruments, or appliances necessary for the practice of a
    trade or profession (Md. Ann. Code of Cts. and Jud. Proc. § 11-504)

PERSONAL PROPERTY
Household furnishings, household goods, wearing apparel, appliances, books, animals kept
    as pets, and other items held for personal, family, or household use to a value of $500
Other property to a value of $5,500 (Md. Ann. Code of Cts. and Jud. Proc. §11-504)

INSURANCE
All money payable on account of sickness, accident, injury, or death of any person (Md.
    Ann. Code of Cts. and Jud. Proc. § 11-504)
A life insurance policy if the beneficiaries are family members (Md. Code. Ann. Art. 48A
    § 385)

PENSIONS
Those received from the retirement systems of state police (Md. Code Ann. Art. 88B § 31
    and 88B § 60), or teachers (Md. Code Ann. Art. 73B § 96), or state employees (Md. Code
    Ann. Art. 73B § 17) and from the Baltimore City Police Department Death Relief Fund (Md.
    Code Ann. Art. 73B § 49)

PUBLIC BENEFITS
Criminal injuries compensation (Md. Code Ann. Art. 26A § 13)
Workmen's compensation (Md. Code Ann. Art. 101 § 50)
Unemployment insurance (Md. Code Ann. Art. 95A § 16)
Public assistance (Md. Code Ann. Art. 88A § 73)

143

MASSACHUSETTS

HOMESTEAD
The homeowner who has a family may claim an exemption of $50,000 (Massachusetts General
    Laws Annotated Chapter 188 § 1)

WAGES
$125 of earned but unpaid wages (Mass. Gen. Laws Ann. Chap. 235 § 34)

TOOLS OF TRADE
Tools, implements, and fixtures necessary for carrying on the debtor's trade or business
    to a value of $500
Materials and stock designed and procured by the debtor and necessary for carrying on his
    or her trade or business to a value of $500
Boats, fishing tackle, and nets of a fisherman to a value of $500
The uniform of an officer or soldier in the militia and the arms and accoutrements
    required by law to be kept by him or her (Mass. Gen. Laws Ann. Chap. 235 § 34)

PERSONAL PROPERTY
Necessary wearing apparel, beds, and bedding for the debtor and his or her family
One heating unit used for warming the dwelling house and cash in an amount not to exceed
    $75 necessary to pay for fuel, heat, water, hot water, and light
Other household furniture to a value of $3,000
Bibles, school books, and library to a value of $200
2 cows, 12 sheep, 2 swine, and 4 tons of hay
Provisions to a value of $300 (or $300 in cash)
A church pew
A burial plot
A sewing machine to a value of $200
Shares in a cooperative association to a value of $100
In lieu of a homestead, cash in an amount not to exceed $200 to pay debtor's monthly rent
In lieu of the exemption for wages, cash or deposits in a banking institution to a value
    of $125
An automobile to a value of $700 (Mass. Gen. Laws Ann. Chap. 235 § 34)
$500 on deposit in a bank or credit union (Mass. Gen. Laws Ann. Chap. 246 § 28A)

INSURANCE
$35 per week payable on account of disability (Mass. Gen. Laws Ann. Chap. 175 § 110A)
A life insurance policy (Mass. Gen. Laws Ann. Chap. 175 § 125)
A group annuity contract (Mass. Gen. Laws Ann. Chap. 175 § 132C)
A group life insurance policy (Mass. Gen. Laws Ann. Chap. 175 § 135)

PENSIONS
100% of pensions received from the retirement system for public employees (Mass. Gen. Laws
    Ann. Chap. 32 § 19)
$100 per week of other pensions (Mass. Gen. Laws Ann. Chap. 246 § 28)

PUBLIC BENEFITS
Public assistance (Mass. Gen. Laws Ann. Chap. 235 § 34)
Workmen's compensation (Mass. Gen. Laws Ann. Chap. 152 § 47)
Unemployment insurance (Mass. Gen. Laws Ann. Chap. 151A § 36)
Veterans' benefits (Mass. Gen. Laws Ann. Chap. 115 § 5)

MICHIGAN

HOMESTEAD
Limitation of value: $3,500
Limitation of area: 1 lot within a town, city, or village, or 40 acres elsewhere (Michigan
    Compiled Laws Annotated § 600.6023)

TOOLS OF TRADE
Tools, implements, materials, stock, apparatus, team, vehicle, motor vehicle, horse,
    harness, or other things to enable the debtor to carry on his or her principal profession,
    trade, occupation, or business to a value of $1,000 (Mich. Com. Laws Ann. § 600.6023)

PERSONAL PROPERTY
All debtors may exempt family pictures, arms, and accoutrements required by law to be kept
    by any person, and wearing apparel, household goods, furniture, utensils, books, and
    appliances to a value of $1,000, a church pew, and a burial plot (Mich. Com. Laws Ann.
    § 600.6023)
In addition, a householder may exempt provisions and fuel for the family for 6 months, 10
    sheep, 2 cows, 5 swine, 100 hens, 5 roosters, and hay and grain to feed said animals for
    6 months. A householder who does not claim the homestead exemption may exempt $1,000
    par value of building and loan association shares (Mich. Com. Laws Ann. § 600.6023)

INSURANCE
Life insurance policies (Mich. Com. Laws Ann. § 500.2207)
Disability insurance (Mich. Com. Laws Ann. § 600.6023)

PENSIONS
Those received from the retirement systems of judges (Mich. Com. Laws Ann. § 38.826),
probate judges (Mich. Com. Laws Ann. § 38.927), legislators (Mich. Com. Laws Ann.
§ 38.1057), state employees (Mich. Com. Laws Ann. § 38.40), municipal employees (Mich.
Com. Laws Ann. § 38.664), public school employees (Mich. Com. Laws Ann. § 38.1346),
state police (Mich. Com. Laws Ann. § 28.110), firemen and policemen (Mich. Com. Laws
Ann. § 38.559)

PUBLIC BENEFITS
Social welfare benefits (Mich. Com. Laws Ann. § 400.63)
Workmen's compensation (Mich. Com. Laws Ann. § 418.821)
Unemployment insurance (Mich. Com. Laws Ann. § 421.30)

MINNESOTA

HOMESTEAD
A debtor may claim real property limited in area to ½ acre within a city or 80 acres elsewhere (Minnesota Statutes Annotated § 510.02), or a mobile home (Minn. Stat. Ann. § 550.37)

WAGES
A minimum of 75% of earned but unpaid wages (for low-income debtors, the exemption may be
higher under a formula based on a multiple of the federal minimum wage)
NOTE: A recipient of relief based on need may exempt 100% of earned but unpaid wages
for six months after he or she returns to employment (Minn. Stat. Ann. § 550.37)

TOOLS OF TRADE
Farm machines and implements, livestock, farm produce, and standing crops to a value of
$5,000
Tools, implements, machines, instruments, office furniture, stock in trade, and library
reasonably necessary in debtor's trade, business, or profession to a value of $5,000
(Minn. Stat. Ann. § 550.37)

PERSONAL PROPERTY
Family Bible, library, musical instruments, church pew, burial plot
Wearing apparel, one watch, household furniture, utensils, household appliances, phono-
graphs, a radio and a television, and food to a total value of $3,000
One motor vehicle to a value of $2,000
Personal injury recoveries (Minn. Stat. Ann. § 550.37)

INSURANCE
A life insurance policy if the beneficiaries are the debtor's spouse and/or children, to a
cash surrender value of $4,000
Insurance claims for damage to exempt property (Minn. Stat. Ann. § 550.37)
Accident or disability insurance benefits (Minn. Stat. Ann. § 550.39)

PENSIONS
Those received from the retirement systems of teachers (Minn. Stat. Ann. §§ 354.10 and
354A.11), public employees (Minn. Stat. Ann. § 353.15), state employees' system (Minn.
Stat. Ann. § 352.15), and highway patrolmen (Minn. Stat. Ann. § 352B.071)
All other pensions to the extent reasonably necessary to support the debtor and his/her
dependents (Minn. Stat. Ann. § 550.37)

PUBLIC BENEFITS
All relief based on need (Minn. Stat. Ann. § 550.37)
Crime victim reparations (Minn. Stat. Ann. § 299B.09)
Veterans' compensation (Minn. Stat. Ann. § 550.38)
Workmen's compensation (Minn. Stat. Ann. § 176.175)
Unemployment insurance (Minn. Stat. Ann. § 268.17)

MISSISSIPPI

HOMESTEAD
A householder may claim real property limited in area to 160 acres and limited in value to
$30,000 (Mississippi Code § 85-3-21)

WAGES
A minimum of 75% of earned but unpaid wages (for low-income debtors, the exemption may be
higher under a formula based on a multiple of the federal minimum wage) (Miss. Code
§ 85-3-4)

TOOLS OF TRADE
Tools of a mechanic necessary for carrying on his or her trade; agricultural implements of
a farmer necessary for two laborers; implements of a laborer necessary in his or her
usual employment; books of a student required for the completion of his or her education;
arms and accoutrements of a member of the militia; globes, maps and other educational
materials used by a teacher; instruments of a surgeon or a dentist used in his or her
profession to a value of $5,000 (Miss. Code § 85-3-1)

145

PERSONAL PROPERTY
Wearing apparel
A library, including pictures, drawings and paintings to a value of $3,000
Family portraits
A sewing machine
Household and kitchen furniture to a value of $5,000
2 work horses or mules and 1 yoke of oxen, 2 cows and calves, 10 hogs, 20 sheep, 20 goats,
  all poultry, all colts under the age of 3 raised in state by the debtor, 250 bushels of
  corn, 10 bushels of wheat or rice, 500 pounds of pork, bacon, or other meat, 100 bushels
  of cottonseed, a wagon, a buggy or cart, one set of harness for each business, 500
  bundles of fodder, 1,000 pounds of hay, 40 gallons of sorghum or molasses or cane syrup,
  1,000 stalks of sugar cane, 1 molasses mill and equipment to value of $250, 2 bridles,
  1 saddle, 1 sidesaddle, and 1 mower and rake for cutting and gathering hay or grain
  (Miss. Code § 85-3-1)
  NOTE: In lieu of the exemptions for tools of trade and personal property, the debtor
         may exempt tangible personal property of any kind to a value of $6,500 (Miss.
         Code § 85-3-1)
Personal injury settlements or judgments to a value of $10,000 (Miss. Code § 85-3-17)

INSURANCE
Insurance claims for damage to exempt property (Miss. Code § 85-3-1)
A $50,000 life insurance policy (Miss. Code § 85-3-11)
Disability insurance (Miss. Code § 85-3-1)

PENSIONS
All pensions from both private (Miss. Code § 71-1-43) and public (Miss. Code § 25-11-129)
  retirement plans

PUBLIC BENEFITS
Workmen's compensation (Miss. Code § 71-3-43)
Unemployment insurance (Miss. Code § 71-5-539)

MISSOURI

HOMESTEAD
Real property to a value of $8000 (Annotated Missouri Statutes §573.475) or a mobile home to
  a value of $1000 (Ann. Mo. Stat. §513.430)

WAGES
A minimum of 75% of earned but unpaid wages (for low-income debtors, the exemption may be
  higher under a formula based on a multiple of the federal minimum wage) (Ann. Mo. Stat.
  §525.030)

TOOLS OF TRADE
Any implements, professional books or tools of trade to a value of $2000 (Ann. Mo. Stat.
  §513.430)

PERSONAL PROPERTY
Household furnishings, household goods, wearing apparel, appliances, books, animals, crops,
  or musical instruments to a value of $1000
Jewelry to a value of $500
A motor vehicle to a value of $500
Wrongful death recoveries
Any other property to a value of $400 (Ann. Mo. Stat. §573.430)
A head of family may exempt any other property to a value of $850 plus $250 for each minor
  child (Ann. Mo. Stat. §513.440)

INSURANCE
Life insurance policies to a loan value of $5000 (Ann. Mo. Stat. §513.430)

PENSIONS
All pensions and annuities to the extent reasonably necessary for the support of the debtor
  and his/her family (Ann. Mo. Stat. §513.430)

146

Social security benefits, unemployment compensation, public assistance, veterans benefits, disability benefits (Ann. Mo. Stat. §513.430)

MONTANA

HOMESTEAD

Limitation of value: $40,000

Limitation of area: 1/4 acre within a town or city, one acre elsewhere (320 acres if used for agricultural purposes) (Montana Code Annotated §70-32-104)

WAGES

100% of earned but unpaid wages if they are necessary for the support of debtor's family (Mont. Code Ann. § 25-13-614)

TOOLS OF TRADE

Heads of families or persons over the age of 60 may take exemptions as follows:
A farmer: farming utensils or implements of husbandry to a value of $600, two oxen or two horses or mules and their harness, one cart or wagon, set of sleds, food for exempt animals for three months, and seed, grain, or vegetables for planting or sowing the following spring to a value of $200.
A mechanic or artisan: tools or implements necessary to carry on debtor's trade
A surgeon, physician, or dentist: instruments and chest necessary to the exercise of debtor's profession, scientific and professional libraries, and necessary office furniture
Attorneys, counselors, judges, ministers of the gospel, editors, school teachers, and music teachers: libraries and necessary office furniture
Music teachers: musical instruments
Notary publics: notarial seal, records, and office furniture
Miners: debtor's cabin or dwelling, sluices, pipes, hose, windlass, derricks, cars, pumps, tools, implements and appliances necessary for mining operations to a value of $1,000, one horse or mule with harness and three months' food for said animal
Civil, mining, or mechanical engineers: instruments, tools, books, and records necessary to carry on debtor's profession
Chemists or assayers: tools, instruments, and supplies necessary to carry on debtor's profession
Cartmen, hackmen, hucksters, peddlers, teamsters, or laborers: one horse or mule and harness for two animals or two oxen and harness, one cart or wagon, one dray or truck, one hack or carriage by which debtor habitually earns a living
Physicians, surgeons, or ministers: one vehicle and harness or other equipment used by debtor in making professional visits and three months' food for a horse, mule, or oxen
Osteopaths or chiropractors: instruments and equipment necessary to the exercise of debtor's profession, scientific and professional library, and necessary office furniture (Mont. Code Ann. § 25-13-612)
Any person may exempt arms, uniforms, and accoutrements required by law to be kept (Mont. Code Ann. § 25-13-613)

PERSONAL PROPERTY

A head of family or person over the age of 60 may exempt:
Wearing apparel
Chairs, tables, desks, and books to a value of $200
Household, table, and kitchen furniture including one sewing machine, stoves, stove pipes, and stove furniture, heating apparatus, beds, bedding, and bedsteads
One clock
All family pictures
Provisions and fuel for three months
One horse, saddle and bridle, 2 cows and their calves, 4 hogs, 50 domestic fowls, feed for exempt animals for 3 months (Mont. Code Ann. § 25-13-611)
A truck or automobile to a value of $1,000 (Mont. Code Ann. § 25-13-617)
One gun (Mont. Code Ann. § 25-13-613)
Other debtors may exempt only their wearing apparel (Mont. Code Ann. § 25-13-611)

INSURANCE

A head of family or person over the age of 60 may exempt life insurance policies if the annual premiums do not exceed $500 (Mont. Code Ann. § 25-13-616)

PENSIONS

100% of pensions received from retirement funds of public employees (Mont. Code Ann. § 19-3-105), teachers (Mont. Code Ann. § 19-4-706), judges (Mont. Code Ann. § 19-5-704), highway patrolmen (Mont. Code Ann. § 19-6-705), sheriffs (Mont. Code Ann. § 19-7-705), game wardens (Mont. Code Ann. § 19-8-805), police officers (Mont. Code Ann. §§ 19-9-1006 and 19-10-504), and firefighters (Mont. Code Ann. §§ 19-11-612 and 19-13-1004)

PUBLIC BENEFITS

Public assistance (Mont. Code Ann. § 53-2-607)
Awards to victims of crime (Mont. Code Ann. § 53-9-129)
Workers' compensation (Mont. Code Ann. § 39-71-743)
Unemployment insurance (Mont. Code Ann. § 39-51-3105)

147

NEBRASKA

HOMESTEAD
A head of family may exempt real property limited in areas to two lots within an incorporated city or village and 160 acres elsewhere and limited in value to $6500 (Revised Statutes of Nebraska §40-101)

WAGES
A head of family may exempt 85% of earned but unpaid wages; others may exempt 75% of earned but unpaid wages. (For low-income debtors, the exemption may be higher under a formula based on a multiple of the federal minimum wage.) (Rev. Stat. of Neb. § 25-1558)

TOOLS OF TRADE
A head of family may exempt all equipment or tools used by the debtor or his/her family for their own support to a value of $1,500 (Rev. Stat. of Neb. § 25-1556)

PERSONAL PROPERTY
Burial Plot (Rev. Stat. of Neb. §12-517)
Immediate personal possessions
Wearing apparel
Kitchen utensils and household furniture to a value of $1,500
Provisions and fuel for six months (Rev. Stat. of Neb. §25-1556)
Personal property other than wages to a value of $2500 if the homestead exemption is not claimed (Rev. Stat. of Neb. §25-1552)

INSURANCE
Life insurance policies, annuities, and accident and health insurance benefits if the beneficiaries are family members (Rev. Stat. of Neb. § 44-371)
Disability insurance benefits --- periodic payments of up to $200 per month (Rev. Stat. of Neb. § 44-754)

PENSIONS
Those received from the retirement systems of county employees (Rev. Stat. of Neb. § 23-2322), state patrolmen (Rev. Stat. of Neb. § 81-2032), school employees (Rev. Stat. of Neb. § 79-1060 and § 79-1552), and state employees (Rev. Stat. of Neb. § 84-1324)
Military disability pensions to a value of $2,000 (Rev. Stat. of Neb. § 25-1559)
For head of family, 85% of other pensions; for others, 75% of other pensions (Rev. Stat. of Neb. § 25-1558)

PUBLIC BENEFITS
Public assistance (Rev. Stat. of Neb. § 68-1013)
Workmen's compensation (Rev. Stat. of Neb. § 48-149)
Unemployment insurance (Rev. Stat. of Neb. § 48-647)

NEVADA

HOMESTEAD
A debtor may exempt either real property or a mobile home limited in value to $75,000 (Nevada Revised Statutes § 115.010)

WAGES
75% of earned but unpaid wages (for low-income debtors, the exemption may be higher under a formula based on a multiple of the federal minimum wage) (Nev. Rev. Stat. § 21.090)

TOOLS OF TRADE
Farm trucks, farm stock, farm tools, farm equipment, supplies, and seed to a value of $4500
Professional libraries, office equipment, office supplies, and the tools, instruments, and materials used to carry on debtor's trade to a value of $4500
The cabin or dwelling of a miner or prospector, cars, implements, and appliances necessary for carrying on mining operations and a mining claim actually worked by the debtor to a value of $4500
All arms, uniforms, and accoutrements required by law to be kept by any person (Nev. Rev. Stat. § 21.090)

PERSONAL PROPERTY
A library to a value of $1500
Family pictures
Keepsakes
Household goods, appliances, furniture, home and yard equipment to a value of $3000
A vehicle to a value of $1000 (Nev. Rev. Stat. § 21.090)

INSURANCE
A life insurance policy if the annual premiums do not exceed $1000 (Nev. Rev. Stat. § 21.090)

PENSIONS
Those received from the public employees' retirement system (Nev. Rev. Stat. § 286.670)

PUBLIC BENEFITS
Aid to dependent children (Nev. Rev. Stat. § 425.210)
SSI (Nev. Rev. Stat. § 427.060)
Industrial insurance (Nev. Rev. Stat. § 616.550)
Unemployment insurance (Nev. Rev. Stat. § 612.710)

NEW HAMPSHIRE

HOMESTEAD
Any debtor may claim real property or manufactured housing to a value of $5,000 (New
  Hampshire Revised Statutes Annotated §480:1)

WAGES
Earned but unpaid wages are exempt under a formula based on a multiple of the federal
  minimum wage (N.H. Rev. Stat. Ann. § 512:21)

TOOLS OF TRADE
Tools of debtor's occupation to a value of $1200
Uniforms, arms, and equipments of a member of the militia (N.H. Rev. Stat. Ann. § 511:2)

PERSONAL PROPERTY
Automobile to a value of $1000
Wearing apparel
Jewelry to a value of $500
Beds, bedsteads, bedding
Household furniture to a value of $2000
Cooking stove, refrigerator, cooking utensils
Sewing machine
Provisions and fuel to a value of $400
Bibles, school books, and a library to a value of $800
One hog and one pig and their pork when slaughtered, six sheep and their fleece, one cow,
  a yoke of oxen or a horse, domestic fowls to a value of $300, four tons of hay
Church pew
Burial plot (N.H. Rev. Stat. Ann. § 511:2)

INSURANCE
Insurance proceeds for damage to exempt property (N.H. Rev. Stat. Ann. § 512:21)

PENSIONS
100% of pensions received from the federal government (N.H. Rev. Stat. Ann. § 512:21)

PUBLIC BENEFITS
Public assistance (N.H. Rev. Stat. Ann. § 167:25)
Workmen's compensation (N.H. Rev. Stat. Ann. § 281:45)
Unemployment insurance (N.H. Rev. Stat. Ann. § 282-A:159)

NEW JERSEY

WAGES
90% of earned but unpaid wages unless the debtor's income is greater than $7,500 per annum
  (New Jersey Statutes Annotated § 2A:17-56)

PERSONAL PROPERTY
Wearing apparel (N.J. Stat. Ann. § 2A:17-19)
Household goods and furniture to a value of $1,000 (N.J. Stat. Ann. § 2A:26-4)
Goods and chattels, shares of stock or interests in any corporation, and personal property
  of every kind to a value (exclusive of wearing apparel) of $1,000 (N.J. Stat. Ann.
  § 2A:17-19)

INSURANCE
Avails of life insurance policies (N.J. Stat. Ann. § 17B:24-6)
Annuities --- periodic payments of up to $500 per month (N.J. Stat. Ann. § 17B:24-7)
Health and disability insurance benefits (N.J. Stat. Ann. § 17B:24-8)
Group life insurance (N.J. Stat. Ann. § 17B:24-9)

PENSIONS
Those received from the pension funds of school district employees (N.J. Stat. Ann.
  § 18A:66-116), prison officers (N.J. Stat. Ann. § 43:7-13), county employees (N.J. Stat.
  Ann. §§ 43:10-14 and 43:10-18.22), municipal employees (N.J. Stat. Ann. §§ 43:13-9, 43:13-
  22.34, 43:13-22.60, and 43:13-44), town employees (N.J. Stat. Ann. § 43:13-37.5), public
  employees (N.J. Stat. Ann. § 43:15A-53), police and firemen (N.J. Stat. Ann. § 43:16-7
  and 43:16A-17), judges (N.J. Stat. Ann. § 43:6A-41), alcoholic beverage control officers
  (N.J. Stat. Ann. § 43:8A-20), officers and employees of city boards of health (N.J. Stat.
  Ann. § 43:18-12), street and water department employees (N.J. Stat. Ann. § 43:19-17),
  and state police (N.J. Stat. Ann. § 53:5A-45)

PUBLIC BENEFITS
Workmen's compensation (N.J. Stat. Ann. § 34:15-29)
Unemployment insurance (N.J. Stat. Ann. § 43:21-15)
Old-age assistance (N.J. Stat. Ann. § 44:7-35)

NEW MEXICO

<u>HOMESTEAD</u>
An individual who is married, widowed, or supporting another may claim real property
   limited in value to $20,000 (New Mexico Statutes Annotated § 42-10-9)

<u>TOOLS OF TRADE</u>
Tools of trade to a value of $1,500 (N.M. Stat. Ann. §§ 42-10-1 and 42-10-2)

<u>PERSONAL PROPERTY</u>
A motor vehicle to a value of $4,000.
Jewelry to a value of $2,500
Clothing
Furniture
Books
Other personal property to a value of $500 (debtors who support only themselves may not
   apply this exemption to money) (N.M. Stat. Ann. §§ 42-10-1 and 42-10-2)
A person who does not claim the homestead exemption may exempt an additional $2,000 of
   personal or real property (N.M. Stat. Ann. § 42-10-10)

<u>INSURANCE</u>
Life insurance policies, annuities, and accident and health insurance benefits (N.M. Stat.
   Ann. § 42-10-3)

<u>PENSIONS</u>
All public and private pension or retirement funds (N.M. Stat. Ann. §§ 42-10-1 and 42-10-2)

<u>PUBLIC BENEFITS</u>
Public assistance (N.M. Stat. Ann. § 27-2-21)
Workers' compensation (N.M. Stat. Ann. § 52-1-52)
Unemployment insurance (N.M. Stat. Ann. § 51-1-37)

NEW YORK

<u>HOMESTEAD</u>
All debtors may claim either real property, an interest in a cooperative apartment or
   condominium, or a mobile home to a value of $10,000 (New York Civil Practice Law and
   Rules § 5206)

<u>WAGES</u>
90% of earned but unpaid wages (100% for some members of the military)(N.Y. Civ. Prac. Law
   and Rules § 5205)

<u>TOOLS OF TRADE</u>
Necessary working tools and implements, including those of a mechanic, farm machinery,
   team, professional instruments, furniture, a library to a value of $600, and food for
   the team for sixty days (N.Y. Civ. Prac. Law and Rules § 5205)

<u>PERSONAL PROPERTY</u>
Wearing apparel
Household furniture, refrigerator, radio, television, crockery, tableware, cooking utensils,
   sewing machine, stoves, and fuel for 60 days
Family Bible, family pictures, school books, and other books to a value of $50
Church pew
Wedding ring and a watch to a value of $35
Food for the family for 60 days
Domestic animals with food for 60 days to a value of $450
Security deposits to a landlord and utility companies
Principal of a trust fund and 90% of the income or other payments to the debtor (N.Y. Civ.
   Prac. Law and Rules § 5205)
A motor vehicle to a value of $2400
Personal injury recoveries to a value of $7500
Wrongful death recoveries (N.Y. Debtor and Creditor Law § 282)
   <u>NOTE</u>: A debtor is limited to an aggregate value of $5000 for all personal property
              exemptions. (N.Y. D. and C. Law § 283). To the extent the debtor does not
              exhaust this $5000 exemption, he or she may exempt cash to a value of $2500
              if the homestead exemption is not claimed (N.Y. D. and C. Law § 284).

<u>INSURANCE</u>
Life insurance policies
Disability insurance benefits --- periodic payments of up to $400 per month
Annuities, if reasonably necessary for the support of debtor and his or her family (N.Y.
   Insurance Law § 166)
Insurance claims for damage to exempt property (N.Y. Civ. Prac. Law and Rules § 5205)

<u>PENSIONS</u>
100% of pensions to the extent necessary to support the debtor and his or her dependents
   (N.Y. D. and C. Law § 282)

<u>PUBLIC BENEFITS</u>
Social Security benefits
Unemployment compensation
Public assistance
Veterans benefits
Crime victim reparations (N.Y. D. and C. Law § 282)

NORTH CAROLINA

A debtor must choose one of the two state exemption systems; the federal exemption system is not allowed.

STATE EXEMPTION SYSTEM #1

HOMESTEAD
A head of family may claim real property limited in value to $1,000 (North Carolina Constitution Article X, § 2)

WAGES
100% of earned but unpaid wages if they are necessary for the support of the debtor's family (General Statutes of North Carolina § 1-362)

PERSONAL PROPERTY
Personal property to a value of $500 (N.C. Const. Art. X, § 1)

INSURANCE
Life insurance policies if the beneficiaries are the debtor's spouse and/or children (N.C. Const. Art. X, § 5)
Group life insurance (Gen. Stat. of N.C. § 58-213)

PENSIONS
Those received from the firemen's relief fund (Gen. Stat. of N.C. § 118-49), and from retirement systems of local government employees (Gen. Stat. of N.C. § 128-31), teachers and state employees (Gen. Stat. of N.C. § 135-9), and law enforcement officers (Gen. Stat. of N.C. § 143-166)

PUBLIC BENEFITS
Public assistance (Gen. Stat. of N.C. § 108A-36)
Workmen's compensation (Gen. Stat. of N.C. § 97-21)
Unemployment insurance (Gen. Stat. of N.C. § 96-17)
Aid to the blind (Gen. Stat. of N.C. § 111-18)

STATE EXEMPTION SYSTEM #2

HOMESTEAD
Real or personal property used as a residence to a value of $7500 (General Statutes of North Carolina § 1C-1601)

TOOLS OF TRADE
Implements, professional books, or tools of trade to a value of $500 (Gen. Stat. of N.C. § 1C-1601)

PERSONAL PROPERTY
A motor vehicle to a value of $1000
Household furnishings, household goods, wearing apparel, appliances, books, animals, crops and musical instruments to a value of $2500 (plus a value of $500 per dependent, not to exceed an additional $2000)
Personal injury and wrongful death recoveries
Other property to a value of $2500 if the homestead exemption is not claimed (Gen. Stat. of N.C. § 1C-1601)

INSURANCE
Life insurance policies if the beneficiaries are the debtor's spouse and/or children (Gen. Stat. of N.C. § 1C-1601)

NORTH DAKOTA

HOMESTEAD
Any debtor may claim real property to a value of $80,000 (North Dakota Century Code § 47-18-01) or a house trailer or mobile home (N.D. Cent. Code § 28-22-02) or, in lieu of the homestead exemption, up to $7,500 (N.D. Cent. Code § 28-22-03.1)

WAGES
A minimum of 75% of earned but unpaid wages (for low-income debtors, the exemption may be higher under a formula based on a multiple of the federal minimum wage) (N.D. Cent. Code § 32-09.1-.03)

PERSONAL PROPERTY
All debtors may exempt:
Family pictures
Church pew
Burial plot
Family Bible, school books, family library to a value of $100
Wearing apparel
Fuel and provisions for one year
Crop and grain raised by the debtor on 160 acres (N.D. Century Code § 28-22-02)
A motor vehicle to a value of $1,200
Wrongful death recoveries to a value of $7,500
Personal injury recoveries to a value of $7,500 (N.D. Cent. Code § 28-22-03.1)

If the debtor is a head of household and does not claim exempt crops, he or she may exempt either additional personal property to a value of $5,000 (N.D. Cent. Code § 28-22-03) or the following additional property:
Books and musical instruments to a value of $1,500
Household and kitchen furniture, including beds, bedsteads, and bedding to a value of $1,000

Livestock and farm implements to a value of $4,500
Tools and implements of a mechanic used in carrying on a trade or business, and stock in
  trade to a value of $1,000
Library and instruments of a professional to a value of $1,000 (N.D. Cent. Code § 28-22-04)

If the debtor is not a head of household and does not claim exempt crops, he or she may
  exempt additional personal property to a value of $2,500 (N.D. Cent. Code § 28-22-05)

INSURANCE
A life insurance policy to a cash surrender value of $4,000 (N.D. Cent. Code § 28-22-03.1)
Life insurance policies if the beneficiaries are the debtor's spouse, children, and/or
  dependents (N.D. Cent. Code § 26-10-17)
Insurance proceeds for damage to exempt property (N.D. Cent. Code § 28-22-02)

PENSIONS
100% of pensions received from the retirement or pension funds of teachers (N.D. Cent.
  Code § 15-39.1-13), firemen (N.D. Cent. Code § 18-05-11), highway patrolmen (N.D. Cent.
  Code § 39-03.1-23), city police officers (N.D. Cent. Code § 40-45-23), city employees
  (N.D. Cent. Code § 40-46-22), and other public employees (N.D. Cent. Code § 54-52-12)
75% of other pensions (N.D. Cent. Code § 32-09.1-03)

PUBLIC BENEFITS
Aid to dependent children (N.D. Cent. Code § 50-09-15)
Workmen's compensation (N.D. Cent. Code § 65-05-29)
Unemployment insurance (N.D. Cent. Code § 52-06-30)

OHIO

HOMESTEAD
Real or personal property used as a residence to a value of $5,000 (Ohio Revised Code
  § 2329.66)

WAGES
75% of earned but unpaid wages (for low-income debtors, the exemption may be higher under
  a formula based on a multiple of the federal minimum wage) (Ohio Rev. Code § 2329.66)

TOOLS OF TRADE
Implements, professional books or tools of debtor's trade or business, including agriculture, to a value of $750 (Ohio Rev. Code § 2329.66)

PERSONAL PROPERTY
A motor vehicle to a value of $1,000
Wearing apparel, beds and bedding to a value of $200 per item
One cooking unit and one refrigerator to a value of $300 each
Cash on hand, money due and payable, tax refunds, money on deposit with a bank, building
  and loan association, savings and loan association, credit union, public utility or
  landlord to a value of $400
Burial plot
Household furnishings, household goods, appliances, books, animals, crops, musical
  instruments, firearms, and hunting and fishing equipment to a value of $200 per item
Jewelry to a value of $400 in one item and $200 in all other items
Wrongful death recoveries
Personal injury recoveries to a value of $5,000
Any other property to a value of $400 (Ohio Rev. Code §2329.66)
> NOTE: The total exemption for household furnishings, etc., and jewelry is $1,500 ($2,000
>   if the homestead exemption is not claimed).

INSURANCE
Avails of life insurance policies if the beneficiaries are the debtor's spouse, children,
  and/or dependents (Ohio Rev. Code § 3911.10)
Group life insurance (Ohio Rev. Code § 3917.05)
Disability insurance benefits --- periodic payments of up to $600 per month (Ohio Rev.
  Code § 3923.19)

PENSIONS
Those received from the retirement systems of public employees (Ohio Rev. Code § 145.560),
  firemen and policemen (Ohio Rev. Code § 146.13 and § 742.47), public school employees
  (Ohio Rev. Code § 3309.66) and § 3307.71), state highway patrolmen (Ohio Rev. Code
  § 5505.22), and most other pensions (Ohio Rev. Code § 2329.66)

PUBLIC BENEFITS
Aid to dependent children (Ohio Rev. Code § 5107.12)
Workmen's compensation (Ohio Rev. Code § 4123.67)
Unemployment insurance (Ohio Rev. Code § 4141.32)
Poor relief payments (Ohio Rev. Code § 5113.01)
Crime victim reparations (Ohio Rev. Code § 2743.66)

OKLAHOMA

HOMESTEAD
A debtor may claim real property limited in value to $5,000 and limited in area to 1 acre
  within a city, town, or village and 160 acres elsewhere. He or she is entitled to claim
  ¼ acre regardless of value (Oklahoma Statutes Annotated Title 31 § 2)

WAGES
75% of earned but unpaid wages (Okla. Stat. Ann. Tit. 31 § 1)

TOOLS OF TRADE
Implements of husbandry used upon the homestead
Tools, apparatus, and books used in a trade or profession (Okla. Stat. Ann. Tit. 31 § 1)

PERSONAL PROPERTY
Household and kitchen furniture
Burial plot
Books, portraits, and pictures
Wearing apparel
One motor vehicle to a value of $1,500
5 milk cows and their calves under the age of 6 months, 100 chickens, 2 horses, 2 bridles and 2 saddles, 10 hogs, and 20 sheep, provisions for the family and forage for exempt livestock for one year
One gun
Personal injury, wrongful death, or workers compensation recoveries to a value of $50,000 (Okla. Stat. Ann. Tit. 31 § 1)

INSURANCE
Life insurance policies (Okla. Stat. Ann. Tit. 36 § 3631)
Group life insurance policies (Okla. Stat. Ann. Tit. 36 § 3632)

PENSIONS
100% of pensions received from the teachers' retirement system (Okla. Stat. Ann. Tit. 70 § 17-109), firemen's relief and pension fund (Okla. Stat. Ann. Tit. 11 § 49-126), police pension and retirement system (Okla. Stat. Ann. Tit. 11 § 50-124), public employees' retirement fund (Okla. Stat. Ann. Tit. 74 § 923), military disability pensions (Okla. Stat. Ann. Tit. 31 § 7), and private retirement, pension, or profit-sharing plans (Okla. Stat. Ann. Tit. 60 § 327)

PUBLIC BENEFITS
Workers' compensation (Okla. Stat. Ann. Tit. 85 § 48)
Unemployment insurance (Okla. Stat. Ann. Tit. 40 § 2-303)
Public assistance (Okla. Stat. Ann. Tit. 56 § 173)

OREGON

HOMESTEAD
A mobile home or real property limited in area to one block within a town or city or 160 acres elsewhere and limited in value to $15,000 ($20,000 aggregate for family members) (Oregon Revised Statutes §§23.164 and 23.240)

WAGES
A minimum of 75% of earned but unpaid wages (for low income debtors, the exemption may be higher under a formula based on a multiple of the federal minimum wage) (Ore. Rev. Stat. § 23.185)

TOOLS OF TRADE
Tools, implements, apparatus, team, harness or library necessary to enable the debtor to carry on the trade, occupation or profession by which he or she habitually earns a living to a value of $750 (Ore. Rev. Stat. § 23.160)

PERSONAL PROPERTY
All debtors may exempt:
Books, pictures and musical instruments to a value of $300
Wearing apparel, jewelry and other personal items to a value of $900
A vehicle to a value of $1200
Household goods, furniture, radios, a television set and utensils to a value of $1450
Domestic animals and poultry kept for family use to a value of $1000 together with food for said animals for 60 days
Personal injury recoveries to a value of $7500
Other personal property to a value of $400 (Ore. Rev. Stat. §23.160)
One rifle or shotgun and one pistol (Ore. Rev. Stat. §23.200)
In addition, a householder may exempt provisions and fuel for 60 days (Ore. Rev. Stat. § 23.160)

INSURANCE
A life insurance policy (Ore. Rev. Stat. § 743.099)
Group life insurance (Ore. Rev. Stat. § 743.102)
Annuities --- periodic payments of up to $250 per month (Ore. Rev. Stat. § 743.105)
Health and disability insurance benefits (Ore. Rev. Stat. § 743.108)

PENSIONS
All public and private pensions (Ore. Rev. Stat. § 23.170)

PUBLIC BENEFITS
General assistance (Ore. Rev. Stat. § 411.760)
Aid to the blind (Ore. Rev. Stat. § 412.115) and the disabled (Ore. Rev. Stat. § 412.610)
Old-age assistance (Ore. Rev. Stat. § 413.130)
Workers' compensation (Ore. Rev. Stat. § 656.234)
Unemployment insurance (Ore. Rev. Stat. § 657.855)
Crime victim reparations (Ore. Rev. Stat. § 23.164)

PENNSYLVANIA

WAGES
100% of earned but unpaid wages (Pennsylvania Consolidated Statutes Annotated Title 42
§ 8127)

PERSONAL PROPERTY
Wearing apparel, Bibles, school books, sewing machine, uniforms, and accoutrements (Pa.
Con. Stat. Ann. Tit. 42 § 8124)
Other real or personal property to a value of $300 (Pa. Con. Stat. Ann. Tit. 42 § 8123)

INSURANCE
Life insurance policies if the beneficiaries are the debtor's spouse, children, and/or
dependents
Annuities --- periodic payments of up to $100 per month
Group life insurance policies
Accident or disability insurance benefits (Pa. Con. Stat. Ann. Tit. 42 § 8124)

PENSIONS
Those received from the retirement or pension systems of public school employees (Pa. Con.
Stat. Ann. Tit. 24 § 8533), state employees (Pa. Con. Stat. Ann. Tit. 71 § 5953), police
(Pa. Con. Stat. Ann. Tit. 53 §§ 764, 776, and 23666), city employees (Pa. Con. Stat. Ann.
Tit. 53 §§ 13445, 23572, and 39383), municipal employees (Pa. Con. Stat. Ann. Tit. 53
§ 881.115), county employees (Pa. Con. Stat. Ann. Tit. 16 § 4716), private employees and
self-employed persons (Pa. Con. Stat. Ann. Tit. 42 § 8124)

PUBLIC BENEFITS
Workers' compensation (Pa. Con. Stat. Ann. Tit. 42 § 8124)
Unemployment insurance (Pa. Con. Stat. Ann. Tit. 43 § 863)

RHODE ISLAND

WAGES
100% of earned but unpaid wages due a seaman or any debtor who has received relief within
the last year
$50 of earned but unpaid wages for other debtors (General Laws of Rhode Island § 9-26-4)

TOOLS OF TRADE
Working tools necessary for the debtor's usual occupation to a value of $500
Professional library of any professional in actual practice
Uniform, arms, ammunition, and equipments of a member of the military (Genl. Laws of R.I.
§ 9-26-4)

PERSONAL PROPERTY
All debtors may exempt:
Wearing apparel
Bibles, school books, other books to a value of $300
Arms, ammunition, and equipments
Church pew
Burial plot
Debts secured by promissory notes
In addition, a housekeeper may exempt:
Household furniture and family stores, including beds and bedding to a value of $1,000
One cow, one and a half tons of hay, one hog and one pig, and the pork of same when
slaughtered (Genl. Laws of R.I. § 9-26-4)

INSURANCE
Avails of life insurance policies (Genl. Laws of R.I. § 27-4-11)
Accident and sickness insurance benefits (Genl. Laws of R.I. § 27-18-24)

PENSIONS
Police and firemen's pensions (Genl. Laws of R.I. § 9-26-5)

PUBLIC BENEFITS
Public assistance (Genl. Laws of R.I. § 40-6-14)
State disability insurance benefits (Genl. Laws of R.I. § 28-41-32)
Workers' compensation (Genl. Laws of R.I. § 28-33-27)
Unemployment insurance (Genl. Laws of R.I. § 28-44-58)

SOUTH CAROLINA

HOMESTEAD
Real or personal property used as a residence to a value of $5000) ($10,000 aggregate for family
members (Code of Laws of South Carolina § 15-41-200)

154

TOOLS OF TRADE
Implements, professional books, or tools of trade to a value of $750 (Code of Laws of S.C. § 15-41-200)

PERSONAL PROPERTY
A motor vehicle to a value of $1200
Household furnishings, household goods, wearing apparel, appliances, books, animals, crops or
    musical instruments to a value of $2500
Jewelry to a value of $500
Cash and other liquid assets to a value of $1000 if the homestead exemption is not claimed
Personal injury and wrongful death recoveries (Code of Laws of S.C. § 15-41-200)

INSURANCE
Life insurance to a cash surrender value of $4000 (Code of Laws of S.C. § 15-41-200)

PENSIONS
All public and private pensions (Code of Laws of S.C. § 15-41-200)

PUBLIC BENEFITS
Social security benefits
Unemployment compensation
Public assistance
Veterans' benefits
Disability benefits
Crime victim reparations (Code of Laws of S.C. § 15-41-200)

SOUTH DAKOTA

HOMESTEAD
A debtor may claim a family homestead consisting of either real property limited in area
    to one acre within a town and 160 acres elsewhere or a mobile home (South Dakota Codi-
    fied Laws §43-31-4)

WAGES
100% of earned but unpaid wages if they are necessary for the use of the family (S.D. Cod.
    Laws § 15-20-12)

PERSONAL PROPERTY
All debtors may exempt:
Family pictures, church pew, burial plot, family Bible, school books, and a family library
    to a value of $200
Wearing apparel
Provisions and fuel for one year (S.D. Cod. Laws § 43-45-2)
In addition, a head of family may exempt additional personal property to a value of $1,500.
    Other debtors may exempt additional personal property to a value of $600 (S.D. Cod. Laws
    § 43-45-4)
In lieu of this exemption, a head of family may exempt:
Books and musical instruments to a value of $200
Household and kitchen furniture, including beds, bedsteads, and bedding to a value of $200
2 cows, 5 swine, 2 yoke of oxen or 1 span of horses or mules, 25 sheep and their lambs
    under the age of 6 months, and all of said sheep's wool and the cloth or yarn
    manufactured therefrom
Food for exempt animals for one year
One wagon, one sleigh, two plows, one harrow, and farming machinery and utensils, including
    tackle for teams, to a value of $1,250
Tools and implements of a mechanic used for his or her trade or business, and stock in
    trade to a value of $200
Library and instruments of a professional to a value of $300 (S.D. Cod. Laws § 43-45-4)

INSURANCE
A life insurance policy with a cash surrender value of $20,000 and health insurance
    benefits to a value of $20,000 (S.D. Cod. Laws § 58-12-4)
Annuities --- periodic payments of up to $250 per month (S.D. Cod. Laws § 58-12-8)

PUBLIC BENEFITS
Workers' compensation (S.D. Cod. Laws § 62-4-42)
Unemployment insurance (S.D. Cod. Laws § 61-6-28)

TENNESSEE

HOMESTEAD
Limitation in value: $5,000 ($7,500 for a married couple) (Tennessee Code Annotated
    § 26-2-301)

WAGES
75% of earned but unpaid wages (for low-income debtors, the exemption may be higher under
    a formula based on a multiple of the federal minimum wage) (Tenn. Code Ann. § 26-2-106)

TOOLS OF TRADE
Implements, professional books, or tools of trade to a value of $750 (Tenn. Code Ann.
    § 26-2-111)

PERSONAL PROPERTY
Burial plot (Tenn. Code Ann. § 26-2-305)
Wearing apparel, family portraits and pictures, family Bible, school books (Tenn. Code Ann. § 26-2-103)
Personal injury recoveries to a value of $7,500 and wrongful death recoveries to a value of $10,000 (Tenn. Code Ann. § 26-2-111)
Other personal property to a value of $4,000 (Tenn. Code Ann. § 26-2-102)

INSURANCE
Accident and disability insurance benefits (Tenn. Code Ann. § 26-2-110)
Life insurance policies if the beneficiaries are the debtor's spouse, children, and/or dependents (Tenn. Code Ann. § 56-7-203)

PENSIONS
100% of pensions received from the state or local government (Tenn. Code Ann. § 26-2-104)
75% of all other pensions (Tenn. Code Ann. § 26-2-106)

PUBLIC BENEFITS
Old-age assistance (Tenn. Code § 14-2-116)
Aid to dependent children (Tenn. Code Ann. § 14-8-121), the disabled (Tenn. Code Ann. § 14-16-112), and the blind (Tenn. Code Ann. § 14-13-117)
Workmen's compensation (Tenn. Code Ann. § 50-1016)
Unemployment insurance (Tenn. Code Ann. § 50-1349)
Social Security and veterans' benefits (Tenn. Code Ann. § 26-2-111)
Crime victim awards to a value of $5,000 (Tenn. Code Ann. § 26-2-111)

TEXAS

HOMESTEAD
A head of family may claim real property located within a city, town, or village limited to a value of $10,000 or real property elsewhere limited in area to 200 acres
A single debtor may claim real property located within a city, town, or village limited to a value of $10,000 or real property elsewhere limited in area to 100 acres (Texas Property Code Annotated §41.001)

WAGES
100% of earned but unpaid wages (Texas Prop. Code Ann. §42.002)

TOOLS OF TRADE
Implements of farming or ranching
Tools, equipment, apparatus (including a boat), and books used in any trade or profession (Texas Prop. Code. Ann. §42.002)

PERSONAL PROPERTY
A debtor may exempt the following property limited to a value of $30,000 for a head of family and $15,000 for a single person when combined with wages, tools of trade, and insurance exemptions:
Home furnishings
Family heirlooms
Provisions
Wearing apparel
Two firearms
Athletic and sporting equipment
5 cows and their calves, 1 breeding-age bull, 20 hogs, 20 sheep, 20 goats, 50 chickens, 30 turkeys, 30 ducks, 30 geese, 30 guineas, and forage for the exempt livestock and fowl
Household pets
All passenger cars and light trucks not held for the production of income, or any two of the following: two animals with saddle and bridle for each (either horses, colts, mules, or donkeys), bicycle or motorcycle, wagon, cart, or dray with harness, auto, truck cab, truck trailer, camper-truck, truck, or pickup truck (Texas Prop. Code Ann. §42.002)

INSURANCE
Cash surrender value of any life insurance policy in force for more than two years if the beneficiaries are members of the family or dependents (Texas Prop. Code Ann. §42.002)
Periodic payments of life, health, or accident insurance benefits (Ann. Stat. of Texas Ins. Code Art. 21.22)

PENSIONS
100% of pensions received from retirement system for state employees (Ann. Stat. of Texas Tit. 110B § 21.005), policemen's relief and retirement fund (Ann. Stat. of Texas Tit. 109 Art. 6243d-1, 6243g-1 and 6243j), firemen's relief and retirement fund (Ann. Stat. of Texas Tit. 109 Art. 6243e, 6243e.1, and 6243e.2), municipal retirement system (Ann. Stat. of Texas Tit. 109 Art. 6243g and Tit. 110B § 61.006), judicial retirement system (Ann. Stat. of Texas Tit. 110B § 41.004), county and district retirement system (Ann. Stat. of Texas Tit. 110B § 51.006), teacher retirement system (Ann. Stat. of Texas Tit. 110B § 31.005) and assistance to survivors of law enforcement officers (Ann. Stat. of Texas Tit. 109 Art. 6228f § 8)

PUBLIC BENEFITS
Workmen's compensation (Ann. Stat. of Texas Tit. 130 Art. 8306 § 3)
Unemployment insurance (Ann. Stat. of Texas Tit. 83 Art. 5221b-13)

UTAH

<u>HOMESTEAD</u>
A debtor may claim real property or a mobile home to a value of $8,000 together with an additional $2,000 for a spouse and $500 for each other dependent (Utah Code § 78-23-3)

<u>TOOLS OF TRADE</u>
Implements, professional books, or tools of trade to a value of $1,500
One motor vehicle to a value of $1,500 if it is used for the debtor's business or profession (Utah Code § 78-23-8)

<u>PERSONAL PROPERTY</u>
Burial plot
One clothes washer and dryer, one freezer, one stove, one sewing machine, all carpets, provisions for three months, wearing apparel (not including jewelry or furs), beds and bedding
Works of art depicting or produced by the debtor and/or family
Personal injury and wrongful death recoveries (Utah Code § 78-23-5)
Furnishings and appliances to a value of $500
Animals, books, and musical instruments to a value of $500
An heirloom or other item of particular sentimental value (Utah Code § 78-23-8)

<u>INSURANCE</u>
Life insurance policies to a cash surrender value of $1,500 (Utah Code § 78-23-7)
Health and disability insurance benefits (Utah Code § 78-23-5)
Insurance claims for damage to exempt property (Utah Code § 78-23-9)

<u>PENSIONS</u>
100% of pensions received from the retirement systems of firemen (Utah Code § 49-6a-36), judges (Utah Code § 49-7a-33), state employees (Utah Code § 49-10-48), public safety employees (Utah Code § 49-11-43), and school employees (Utah Code §§ 53-29-46 and 53-29-56), and 100% of other pensions if necessary for the support of the debtor and his/her dependents (Utah Code § 78-23-6)

<u>PUBLIC BENEFITS</u>
Public assistance (Utah Code § 55-15-32)
Workmen's compensation (Utah Code § 35-1-80)
Unemployment insurance (Utah Code § 35-4-18)

VERMONT

<u>HOMESTEAD</u>
Limitation in value: $30,000 (Vermont Statutes Annotated Title 27 § 101)

<u>TOOLS OF TRADE</u>
Professional books and instruments of physicians and dentists to a value of $200
Professional books of clergy and attorneys to a value of $200
Tool chest of a mechanic (Vt. Stat. Ann. Tit. 12 § 2740)

<u>PERSONAL PROPERTY</u>
Apparel, bedding, tools, arms, articles of household furniture, sewing machine, Bibles and other books, church pew
1 cow to a value of $100, 1 swine or its meat, 10 sheep to a value of $100, 1 year's product of such sheep in wool, yarn, or cloth, forage for 10 sheep, 1 cow, and 2 oxen or horses through 1 winter, and live poultry to a value of $10
10 cords of firewood or 5 tons of coal
Growing crops, 20 bushels of potatoes, 10 bushels of grain, 1 barrel of flour, 3 swarms of bees and their hives with their honey, 200 pounds of sugar
1 yoke of oxen or steers or 2 horses for team work to a value of $300, a wagon or oxcart, a sled or set of sleds for oxen or horses, 2 harnesses, 2 halters, 2 chains, 1 plow and 1 ox yoke to a value, together with the team of oxen, steers, or horses, of $350
Pistols, sidearms, and equipment of a soldier or his heirs kept as mementos of his service (Vt. Stat. Ann. Tit. 12 § 2740)

<u>PENSIONS</u>
100% of pensions received from the state employees retirement system (Vt. Stat. Ann. Tit. 3 § 476), state teachers (Vt. Stat. Ann. Tit. 16 § 1946), and municipal employees (Vt. Stat. Ann. Tit. 24 § 5066)

<u>PUBLIC BENEFITS</u>
Public assistance (Vt. Stat. Ann. Tit. 33 § 2575)
Workmen's compensation (Vt. Stat. Ann. Tit. 21 § 681)
Unemployment insurance (Vt. Stat. Ann. Tit. 21 § 1367)

VIRGINIA

<u>WAGES</u>

A minimum of 75% of earned but unpaid wages (for low-income debtors, the exemption may be higher under a formula based on a multiple of the federal minimum wage) (Code of Virginia § 34-29)

<u>TOOLS OF TRADE</u>

Mechanics: tools and utensils of trade
Oystermen or fishermen: boat and tackle to a value of $1,500 (Code of Va. § 34-26)
Persons engaged in agriculture: a pair of horses or mules with necessary gearing, one wagon or cart, one tractor to a value of $3,000, two plows, one drag, one harvest cradle, one pitchfork, one rake, two iron wedges, fertilizer to a value of $1,000 (Code of Va. § 34-27)

<u>PERSONAL PROPERTY</u>

A householder may exempt:
Family Bible
Wedding and engagement rings
Family pictures, school books, and library
Burial plot
Wearing apparel
Beds, bedsteads, bedding
Two dressers or two dressing tables, wardrobes, chifforobes or chests of drawers, or a dresser and one dressing table
Carpets, rugs, linoleum, or other floor covering
3 stoves and appendages
6 chairs, 6 plates, 1 table, 12 knives, 12 forks, 24 spoons, 12 dishes, 2 basins, 1 pot, 1 oven, 6 pieces of wooden- or earthenware
One dining-room table, one buffet, one china press
One cooking stove and utensils, one icebox freezer or refrigerator, one washing machine, one clothes dryer to a value of $150, one sewing machine, one loom and its appurtenances, one spinning wheel, one pair of cards, one kitchen safe or one kitchen cabinet or press
One ax, two hoes
All cats, dogs, birds, squirrels, rabbits, and other pets
One cow and her calf under one year of age, one horse, three hogs, fowl to a value of $25, forage or hay to a value of $25
50 bushels of corn or 25 bushels of rye or buckwheat, 5 bushels of wheat or one barrel of flour, 20 bushels of potatoes, 200 pounds of bacon or pork, all canned and frozen goods, other provisions to a value of $50 (Code of Va. § 34-26)
Other real and personal property to a value of $5,000 (Code of Va. § 34-4)
  <u>NOTE</u>: Disabled veterans may exempt other real and personal property to a value of $2,000 (Code of Va. § 34-4.1)
Written declaration of the intent to claim the exemption as to real property must be recorded prior to bankruptcy (Code of Va. § 34-6)

<u>INSURANCE</u>

A head of household may exempt a $10,000 life insurance policy (Code of Va. § 38.1-449)
All debtors may exempt group life insurance policies (Code of Va. § 38.1-482) and industrial sick insurance benefits (Code of Va. § 38.1-488)

<u>PENSIONS</u>

100% of pensions received from the state supplemental retirement system (Code of Va. § 51-111.15), certain county, city, and town employees' pension funds (Code of Va. § 51-127.7), and judicial retirement system (Code of Va. § 51-180)
75% of other pensions (Code of Va. § 34-29)

<u>PUBLIC BENEFITS</u>

Awards to victims of crime (Code of Va. § 19.2-368.12)
Workmen's compensation (Code of Va. § 65.1-82)
Unemployment insurance (Code of Va. § 60.1-125)

WASHINGTON

<u>HOMESTEAD</u>

Limitation of value: $25,000 (Revised Code of Washington Annotated §6.12.050)

<u>WAGES</u>

A minimum of 75% of earned but unpaid wages (for low-income debtors, the exemption may be higher under a formula based on a multiple of the state minimum wage) (Rev. Code of Wash. Ann. §7.33.280)

<u>TOOLS OF TRADE</u>

A farmer may exempt farm trucks, farm stock, farm tools, farm equipment, supplies, and seed to a value of $3,000
A physician, surgeon, attorney, clergyman or other professional may exempt a library, office furniture, office equipment, and supplies to a value of $3,000
Any other person may exempt tools and instruments and materials used to carry on a trade to a value of $3,000 (Rev. Code of Wash. Ann. §6.16.020)

PERSONAL PROPERTY
Wearing apparel --- not to exceed a value of $750 in furs, jewelry, and personal ornaments
    for any person; private libraries to a value of $1,000; family pictures and keepsakes
Household goods, appliances, furniture, and home and yard equipment to a value of $1,500
Provisions and fuel for three months
A motor vehicle to a value of $1,200
Other property to a value of $500 (no more than $100 can be in the form of cash, bank accounts,
    savings and loan accounts, stocks, bonds or other securities) (Rev. Code of Wash. Ann. § 6.16.020)

INSURANCE
Disability insurance benefits (Rev. Code of Wash. Ann. § 48.18.400)
Life insurance policies (Rev. Code of Wash. Ann. § 48.18.410)
Group life insurance policies (Rev. Code of Wash. Ann. § 48.18.420)
Annuities --- periodic payments of up to $250 per month (Rev. Code of Wash. Ann.
    § 48.18.430)

PENSIONS
Those received from the federal government (Rev. Code of Wash. Ann. §6.16.030), public
    employees retirement fund (Rev. Code of Wash. Ann. §41.40.380) and state patrol retire-
    ment fund (Rev. Code of Wash. Ann. §43.43.310)

PUBLIC BENEFITS
Public assistance (Rev. Code of Wash. Ann. § 74.04.280)
Workmen's compensation (Rev. Code of Wash. Ann. § 51.32.040)
Unemployment insurance (Rev. Code of Wash. Ann. § 50.40.020)

WEST VIRGINIA

HOMESTEAD
Limitation in value: $7,500 (West Virginia Code § 38-10-4)

TOOLS OF TRADE
Implements, professional books or tools of trade to a value of $750 (W. Va. Code § 38-10-4)

PERSONAL PROPERTY
A motor vehicle to a value of $1,200
Household furnishings, household goods, wearing apparel, appliances, books, animals, crops,
    and musical instruments to a total value of $1,000 (no more than $200 per item)
Jewelry to a value of $500
Personal injury recoveries to a value of $7,500
Wrongful death recoveries
Other property to a value of $400 ($7,900 if the homestead is not claimed) (W. Va. Code
    § 38-10-4)

INSURANCE
A life insurance policy with a cash surrender value of $4,000
Health and disability insurance benefits (W. Va. Code § 38-10-4)

PENSIONS
All pensions to the extent reasonably necessary for the support of the debtor and his/her
    dependents (W. Va. Code § 38-10-4)

PUBLIC BENEFITS
Public assistance (W. Va. Code § 38-10-4)
Unemployment insurance (W. Va. Code § 38-10-4)
Crime victim awards (W. Va. Code § 38-10-4)
Veterans' benefits (W. Va. Code § 38-10-4)
Social Security (W. Va. Code § 38-10-4)

WISCONSIN

HOMESTEAD
Any debtor may claim real property to a value of $25,000 (Wisconsin Statutes Annotated
    § 815.20)

WAGES
A person with no dependents may exempt 60% of earned but unpaid wages, not less than $75
    nor more than $100
A person with dependents may exempt $120 plus $20 for each dependent, not to exceed 75% of
    earned but unpaid wages (Wis. Stat. Ann. § 815.18)

TOOLS OF TRADE
Tools, implements, and stock in trade of a mechanic, miner, merchant, trader, or other
    person to a value of $200
Printing materials and press or presses used in the business of any printer or publisher
    to a value of $1,500
Uniform, arms, and equipments of members of the state national guard
Books, maps, plats and other papers used for making abstracts of title to land (Wis. Stat.
    Ann. § 815.18)

PERSONAL PROPERTY
Family Bible, family pictures, school books, library
Church pew
Burial plot
Wearing apparel
Jewelry and other articles of adornment to a value of $400
Television, radio
Beds, bedsteads, bedding
Stoves and appendages
Cooking utensils and household furniture to a value of $200
Sewing machine
U.S. Savings Bonds to a value of $200
Savings and loan, bank, or credit union accounts to a value of $1,000 if no homestead is
    claimed
Patents
Provisions and fuel for one year
One gun, rifle, or other firearm to a value of $50
One automobile to a value of $1,000
8 cows, 10 swine, 50 chickens, 2 horses or 2 mules, 10 sheep and their wool, food for
    exempt stock for 1 year
One wagon, cart, or dray, one sleigh, one plow, one drag, one binder, one tractor to a
    value of $1,500, one corn binder, one mower, one springtooth harrow, one disc harrow,
    one seeder, one hay loader, one corn planter, one set of heavy harness, other farming
    utensils to a value of $300 (Wis. Stat. Ann. § 815.18)

INSURANCE
Life insurance policies
Disability insurance benefits to a value of $150 per month
Insurance claims for fire damage to exempt property (Wis. Stat. Ann. § 815.18)

PENSIONS
100% of veterans' benefits, military pensions, retirement, pension, stock bonus, or
    profit-sharing plans of private employers and self-employed persons' retirement arrange-
    ments (Wis. Stat. Ann. § 815.18) and 100% of pensions received from fire and police
    pension fund (Wis. Stat. Ann. § 815.18), public employees' retirement system (Wis. Stat.
    Ann. § 41.22), state teachers' retirement system (Wis. Stat. Ann. § 42.52), and certain
    city employees' retirement systems (Wis. Stat. Ann. § 66.81)

PUBLIC BENEFITS
Aid to families with dependent children and other payments made for social services (Wis.
    Stat. Ann. § 49.41)
Workmen's compensation (Wis. Stat. Ann. § 102.27)
Unemployment insurance (Wis. Stat. Ann. § 108.13)

WYOMING

HOMESTEAD
Real property or a mobile home limited in value to $10,000 (Wyoming Statutes Annotated
    §1-20-101)

WAGES
50% of earned but unpaid wages if necessary for the use of the debtor's family (Wy. Stat.
    Ann. §1-17-411)

TOOLS OF TRADE
Tools, motor vehicle, team, implements, stock in trade used and kept for the purpose of
    carrying on the debtor's trade or business to a value of $2,000; or
Library, instruments, and implements of a professional to a value of $2,000 (Wy. Stat.
    Ann. §1-20-106)

PERSONAL PROPERTY
Family Bible, pictures, and school books
A burial plot
Furniture, bedding, provisions, and household articles to a value of $2,000 (Wy. Stat.
    Ann. §1-20-106)
Wearing apparel to a value of $1,000 (Wy. Stat. Ann. §1-20-105)

PENSIONS
Those received from the state retirement system (Wy. Stat. Ann. § 9-5-226) and firemen's
    pension fund (Wy. Stat. Ann. § 15-5-209)

PUBLIC BENEFITS
Public assistance (Wy. Stat. Ann. §42-1-114)
Workers' compensation (Wy. Stat. Ann. §27-12-708)
Unemployment insurance (Wy. Stat. Ann. §27-3-319)

160

APPENDIX B

$$$$$

STATES AND CITIES IN WHICH BANKRUPTCY COURTS ARE LOCATED

Alabama: Anniston, Birmingham, Decatur, Mobile, Tuscaloosa

Alaska: Anchorage

Arizona: Phoenix, Tucson

Arkansas: Little Rock

California: Ceres, Eureka, Fresno, Los Angeles, Oakland, Sacramento, San Bernardino, San Diego, San Francisco, San Jose, Santa Ana

Colorado: Denver

Connecticut: Bridgeport, Hartford

Delaware: Wilmington

District of Columbia: Washington, D.C.

Florida: Jacksonville, Miami, Tallahassee, Tampa

Georgia: Atlanta, Columbus, Macon, Savannah

Hawaii: Honolulu

Idaho: Boise

Illinois: Belleville, Chicago, Danville, Springfield

Indiana: Evansville, Gary, Indianapolis, South Bend

Iowa: Cedar Rapids, Des Moines

STATES AND CITIES WITH BANKRUPTCY COURTS

Kansas: Kansas City, Wichita

Kentucky: Lexington, Louisville

Louisiana: Baton Rouge, New Orleans, Opelousas, Shreveport

Maine: Bangor, Portland

Maryland: Baltimore, Hyattsville

Massachusetts: Boston

Michigan: Detroit, Flint, Grand Rapids, Marquette

Minnesota: Duluth, Minneapolis, St. Paul

Mississippi: Greenville, Jackson

Missouri: Kansas City, St. Louis

Montana: Billings

Nebraska: Omaha

Nevada: Las Vegas, Reno

New Hampshire: Manchester

New Jersey: Camden, Newark, Trenton

New Mexico: Albuquerque

New York: Albany, Brooklyn, Buffalo, New York, Poughkeepsie, Rochester, Utica, Westbury, Yonkers

North Carolina: Charlotte, Greensboro, Wilson

North Dakota: Fargo

Ohio: Akron, Canton, Cincinnati, Cleveland, Columbus, Dayton, Toledo, Youngstown

Oklahoma: Oklahoma City, Okmulgee, Tulsa

Oregon: Portland

Pennsylvania: Erie, Philadelphia, Pittsburgh, Reading, Wilkes-Barre

Rhode Island: Providence

South Carolina: Columbia

South Dakota: Sioux Falls

Tennessee: Chattanooga, Jackson, Knoxville, Memphis, Nashville

Texas: Dallas, Fort Worth, Houston, Lubbock, San Antonio, Tyler

Utah: Salt Lake City

Vermont: Rutland

BANKRUPTCY: DO IT YOURSELF

Virginia: Alexandria, Harrisonburg, Lynchburg, Norfolk, Richmond, Roanoke

Washington: Seattle, Spokane

West Virginia: Charleston, Wheeling

Wisconsin: Eau Claire, Madison, Milwaukee

Wyoming: Cheyenne

APPENDIX

BANKRUPTCY
FORMS

Use this form to order more forms.
Send to Nolo Press, 950 Parker St., Berkeley CA 94710.

Send _____ sets of the regular 8½-by-11" forms at $11.50/set. $ _____
California residents add 6½% sales tax (52¢/set of forms). $ _____

                                                          Total $ _____

send to: NOLO PRESS
            950 Parker St.
            Berkeley CA 94710

*In re

CHAPTER 7

**VOLUNTARY CASE:
DEBTOR'S *JOINT* PETITION**[1]

Debtor   Include here all names used by debtor within last 6 years.

(If this form is used for joint petitioners wherever the word "petitioner" or words referring to petitioners are used they shall be read as if in the plural.)

1. Petitioner's post-office address is

2. Petitioner has
   ☐ resided within this district for the preceding 180 days.
   ☐ had his *(her)* domicile within this district for the preceding 180 days.
   ☐ had his *(her)* principal place of business within this district for the preceding 180 days.
   ☐ resided or been domiciled or had his *(her)* principal place of business within this district for a longer portion of the preceding 180 days than in any other district.

3. Petitioner is qualified to file this petition and is entitled to the benefits of title 11, United States Code as a voluntary debtor.

Wherefore, petitioner prays for relief in accordance with chapter 7 of title 11, United States Code.

Signed:..
         Attorney for Petitioner

Address:..

....

Petitioner(s) signs if not represented by attorney

....
         Petitioner

....
         Petitioner

DECLARATION[2]

INDIVIDUAL: I,   the petitioner named in the foregoing petition, certify under penalty of perjury that the foregoing is true and correct.

JOINT INDIVIDUALS: We,   and   the petitioners named in the foregoing petition, certify under penalty of perjury that the foregoing is true and correct.

CORPORATION: I,   the   of the corporation named as petitioner in the foregoing petition, certify under penalty of perjury that the foregoing is true and correct, and that the filing of this petition on behalf of the corporation has been authorized.

PARTNERSHIP: I,   *a member — an authorized agent —* of the partnership named as petitioner in the foregoing petition, certify under penalty of perjury that the foregoing is true and correct, and that the filing of this petition on behalf of the partnership has been authorized.

Executed on   19   Signature:..
         Petitioner

....
         Petitioner

Form Nos. 1 & 2 combined & 5, chapter 7, Voluntary case: debtor's petition individual, joint, corporation and partnership, 10-79.

© 1979 JULIUS BLUMBERG, INC.

Case No.

In re

STATEMENT OF
FINANCIAL AFFAIRS FOR DEBTOR
NOT ENGAGED IN BUSINESS

Debtor   Include here all names used by debtor within last 6 years.

Each question should be answered or the failure to answer explained. If the answer is "none," this should be stated. If additional space is needed for the answer to any question, a separate sheet, properly identified, and made a part hereof, should be used and attached.

The term "original petition," as used in the following questions, shall mean the petition filed under Rule 1002, 1003, or 1004.

(If this form is used by joint debtors wherever the word "debtor" or words referring to debtor are used they shall be read as if in the plural.)

1. Name and residence.

a. What is your full name and social security number?

b. Have you used, or been known by, any other names within the 6 years immediately preceding the filing of the original petition herein?
(If so, give particulars.)

c. Where do you now reside?

d. Where else have you resided during the 6 years immediately preceding the filing of the original petition herein?

2. Occupation and income.

a. What is your occupation?

b. Where are you now employed?
(Give the name and address of your employer, or the address at which you carry on your trade or profession, and the length of time you have been so employed or engaged.)

c. Have you been in a partnership with anyone, or engaged in any business during the 6 years immediately preceding the filing of the original petition herein?
(If so, give particulars, including names, dates, and places.)

d. What amount of income have you received from your trade or profession during each of the 2 calendar years immediately preceding the filing of the original petition herein?

e. What amount of income have you received from other sources during each of these 2 years?
(Give particulars, including each source, and the amount received therefrom.)

3. Tax returns and refunds.

a. Where did you file your federal and state income tax returns for the 2 years immediately preceding the filing of the original petition herein?

b. What tax refunds (income and other) have you received during the year immediately preceding the filing of the original petition herein?

c. To what tax refunds (income or other), if any, are you, or may you be, entitled?
(Give particulars, including information as to any refund payable jointly to you and your spouse or any other person.)

4. Bank accounts and safe deposit boxes.

a. What bank accounts have you maintained alone or together with any other person, and in your own or any other name within the 2 years immediately preceding the filing of the original petition herein?
(Give the name and address of each bank, the name in which the deposit is maintained, and the name and address of every other person authorized to make withdrawals from such account.)

b. What safe deposit box or boxes or other depository or depositories have you kept or used for your securities, cash, or other valuables within the 2 years immediately preceding the filing of the original petition herein?
(Give the name and address of the bank or other depository, the name in which each box or other depository was kept, the name and address of every other person who had the right of access thereto, a brief description of the contents thereof, and, if the box has been surrendered, state when surrendered, or, if transferred, when transferred, and the name and address of the transferee.)

5. Books and records.

a. Have you kept books of account or records relating to your affairs within the 2 years immediately preceding the filing of the original petition herein?

b. In whose possession are these books or records?
(Give names and addresses.)

c. If any of these books or records are not available, explain.

d. Have any books of account or records relating to your affairs been destroyed, lost or otherwise disposed of within the 2 years immediately preceding the filing of the original petition herein?
(If so, give particulars, including date of destruction, loss, or disposition, and reason therefor.)

6. Property held for another person.

What property do you hold for any other person?
(Give name and address of each person, and describe the property, or value thereof, and all writings relating thereto.)

7. Prior bankruptcy.

What proceedings under the Bankruptcy Act or title 11, United States Code have previously been brought by or against you?
(State the location of the bankruptcy court, the nature and number of each case, the date when it was filed, and whether a discharge was granted or refused, the case was dismissed, or a composition, arrangement, or plan was confirmed.)

© 1979 JULIUS BLUMBERG, INC.

8. Receiverships, general assignments, and other modes of liquidation.

a. Was any of your property, at the time of the filing of the original petition herein, in the hands of a receiver, trustee, or other liquidating agent? (If so, give a brief description of the property, the name and address of the receiver, trustee, or other agent, and, if the agent was appointed in a court proceeding, the name and location of the court the title and number of the case, and the nature of the proceeding.)

b. Have you made any assignment of your property for the benefit of your creditors, or any general settlement with your creditors, within one year immediately preceding the filing of the original petition herein?
(If so, give dates, the name and address of the assignee, and a brief statement of the terms of assignment or settlement.)

9. Property in hands of third person.

Is any other person holding anything of value in which you have an interest? (Give name and address, location and description of the property, and circumstances of the holding.)

10. Suits, executions, and attachments.

a. Were you a party to any suit pending at the time of the filing of the original petition herein? (If so, give the name and location of the court and the title and nature of the proceeding.)

b. Were you a party to any suit terminated within the year immediately preceding the filing of the original petition herein.? (If so, give the name and location of the court, the title and nature of the proceeding, and the result.)

c. Has any of your property been attached, garnished, or seized under any legal or equitable process within the year immediately preceding the filing of the original petition herein? (If so, describe the property seized or person garnished, and at whose suit.)

11. Loans repaid.

What repayments on loans in whole or in part have you made during the year immediately preceding the filing of the original petition herein?
(Give the name and address of the lender, the amount of the loan and when received, the amounts and dates of payments and, if the lender is a relative or insider, the relationship.)

12. Transfers of property.

a. Have you made any gifts, other than ordinary and usual presents to family members and charitable donations, during the year immediately preceding the filing of the original petition herein? (If so, give names and addresses of donees and dates, description, and value of gifts.)

b. Have you made any other transfer, absolute or for the purpose of security, or any other disposition, of real or tangible personal property during the year immediately preceding the filing of the original petition herein? (Give a description of the property, the date of the transfer or disposition, to whom transferred or how disposed of, and, if the transferee is a relative or insider, the relationship, the consideration, if any, received therefor, and the disposition of such consideration.)

13. Repossessions and returns.

Has any property been returned to, or repossessed by, the seller or by a secured party during the year immediately preceding the filing of the original petition herein?
(If so, give particulars including the name and address of the party getting the property and its description and value.)

14. Losses.

a. Have you suffered any losses from fire, theft, or gambling during the year immediately preceding or since the filing of the original petition herein? (If so, give particulars, including dates, names, and places, and the amounts of money or value and general description of property lost.)

b. Was the loss covered in whole or part by insurance? (If so, give particulars.)

15. Payments or transfers to attorneys.

a. Have you consulted an attorney during the year immediately preceding or since the filing of the original petition herein? (Give date, name, and address.)

b. Have you during the year immediately preceding or since the filing of the original petition herein paid any money or transferred any property to the attorney or to any other person on his behalf?
(If so, give particulars, including amount paid or value of property transferred and date of payment or transfer.)

c. Have you, either during the year immediately preceding or since the filing of the original petition herein, agreed to pay any money or transfer any property to an attorney at law, or to any other person on his behalf?
(If so, give particulars, including amount and terms of obligation.)

UNSWORN DECLARATION UNDER PENALTY OF PERJURY

and

I *(We)*,

certify under penalty of perjury that I *(we)* have read the foregoing schedules, consisting of   sheets, and that they are true and correct to the best of my *(our)* knowledge, information, and belief.

Executed on   19

....
Signature   Signature

Form No. 7, statement of affairs: not engaged in business: page 2, 10-79

© 1979 JULIUS BLUMBERG. INC.

In re

Debtor   Include here all named used by debtor within last 6 years.

Schedule A — STATEMENT OF ALL LIABILITIES OF DEBTOR

(If this form is used by joint debtors wherever the word "debtor" or words referring to debtor are used they shall be read as if in the plural.)
Schedules A-1, A-2, and A-3 must include all the claims against the debtor(s) or debtors' property as of the date of the filing of the petition by or against debtor.

SCHEDULE A-1 — CREDITORS HAVING PRIORITY

(1) Nature of Claim	(2) Name of creditor and complete mailing address including zip code (if unknown, so state)	(3) Specify when claim was incurred and the consideration therefor; when claim is contingent, unliquidated, disputed, or subject to setoff, evidenced by a judgment, negotiable instrument, or other writing, or incurred as partner or joint contractor, so indicate; specify name of any partner or joint contractor on any debt.	(4) Indicate if claim is contingent, unliquidated or disputed.	(5) Amount of Claim
a. Wages, salary, and commissions, including vacation, severance and sick leave pay owing to workmen, servants, clerks, or traveling or city salesmen on salary or commission basis, whole or part time, whether or not selling exclusively for the debtor, not exceeding $2,000 to each, earned within 90 days before filing of petition or cessation of business, if earlier (specify date).				$
b. Contributions to employee benefit plans for services rendered within 180 days before filing of petition or cessation of business, if earlier (specify date).				
c. Deposits by individuals, not exceeding $900 for each for purchase, lease, or rental of property or services for personal, family, or household use that were not delivered or provided.				
d. Taxes owing (itemize by type of tax and taxing authority:) (1) To the United States (2) To any State (3) To any other taxing authority				
			Total	

© 1979 JULIUS BLUMBERG, INC.

Schedule A-2 — Creditors Holding Security

(1) Name of creditor and complete mailing address including zip code (if unknown, so state)	(2) Description of security and date when obtained by creditor	(3) Specify when claim was incurred and the consideration therefor; when claim is contingent, unliquidated, disputed, subject to setoff, evidenced by a judgment, negotiable instrument, or other writing, or incurred as partner or joint contractor, so indicate; specify name of any partner or joint contractor on any debt.	(4) Indicate if claim is contingent, unliquidated or disputed	(5) Market value	(6) Amount of claim without deduction of value of security
				$	$
None of the above claims is contingent, liquidated or disputed unless otherwise stated.			Total		

Schedule A-3 — Creditors Having Unsecured Claims Without Priority

Name of creditor (including last known holder of any negotiable instrument) complete mailing address including zip code (if unknown, so state).	Specify when claim was incurred and the consideration therefor; when claim is contingent, unliquidated, disputed, subject to setoff, evidenced by a judgment, negotiable instrument, or other writing, or incurred as partner or joint contractor, so indicate; specify name of any partner or joint contractor on any debt.	Amount of Claim
		$
None of the above claims is contingent, liquidated or disputed unless otherwise stated.	Total	

Form No. 6, Schedule A-2 & A-3, 10-79

© 1979 JULIUS BLUMBERG, INC.

Schedule A-3 — Creditors Having Unsecured Claims Without Priority

Name of creditor (including last known holder of any negotiable instrument) complete mailing address including zip code (if unknown, so state).	Specify when claim was incurred and the consideration therefor; when claim is contingent, unliquidated, disputed, subject to setoff, evidenced by a judgment, negotiable instrument, or other writing, or incurred as partner or joint contractor, so indicate; specify name of any partner or joint contractor on any debt	Amount of claim
		$
	Total	

None of the above claims is contingent, liquidated or disputed unless otherwise stated.

© 1979 JULIUS BLUMBERG. INC.

SCHEDULE B — STATEMENT OF ALL PROPERTY OF DEBTOR

Schedules B-1, B-2, B-3, and B-4 must include all property of the debtor as of the date of the filing of the petition by or against debtor.

Schedule B-1 — Real Property

Description and location of all real property in which debtor has an interest (including equitable and future interests, interests in estates by the entirety, community property, life estates, leaseholds, and rights and powers exercisable for the benefit of debtor)	Nature of interest (specify all deeds and written instruments relating thereto)	Market value of debtor's interest without deduction for secured claims listed in schedule A-2 or exemptions claimed in schedule B-4
		$
Total		

Schedule B-2 — Personal Property

Type of Property	Description and location	Market value of debtor's interest without deduction for secured claims listed on schedule A-2 or exemptions claimed in schedule B-4
a. Cash on hand		$
b. Deposits of money with banking institutions, savings and loan associations, credit unions, public utility companies, landlords, and others		
c. Household goods, supplies, and furnishings		
d. Books, pictures, and other art objects; stamp, coin, and other collections		
e. Wearing apparel, jewelry, firearms, sports equipment, and other personal possessions		
f. Automobiles, trucks, trailers, and other vehicles		
g. Boats, motors, and their accessories		
Total		

Form No. 6. Schedule B-1 & B-2. 10-79

© 1979 JULIUS BLUMBERG, INC

Schedule B-2 — Personal Property (Continued)

Type of property	Description and location	Market value of debtor's interest without deduction for secured claims listed on schedule A-2 or exemptions claimed in schedule B-4	
h. Livestock, poultry, and other animals		$	
i. Farming supplies and implements			
j. Office equipment, furnishings, and supplies			
k. Machinery, fixtures, equipment, and supplies (other than those listed in items j and l) used in business			
l. Inventory			
m. Tangible personal property of any other description			
n. Patents, copyrights, franchises, and other general intangibles (specify all documents and writings relating thereto)			
o. Government and corporate bonds and other negotiable and nonnegotiable instruments			
p. Other liquidated debts owing debtor			
q. Contingent and unliquidated claims of every nature, including counterclaims of the debtor (give estimated value of each)			
r. Interests in insurance policies (itemize surrender or refund values of each)			
s. Annuities			
t. Stocks and interests in incorporated and unincorporated companies (itemize separately)			
u. Interests in partnerships			
v. Equitable and future interests, life estates, and rights or powers exercisable for the benefit of the debtor (other than those listed in schedule B-1) [specify all written instruments relating thereto]	Total		

© 1979 JULIUS BLUMBERG, INC.

Schedule B-3 — Property Not Otherwise Scheduled

Type of property	Description and location	Market value of debtor's interest without deduction for secured claims listed in schedule A-2 or exemptions claimed in schedule B-4
a. Property transferred under assignment for benefit of creditors, within 120 days prior to filing of petition (specify date of assignment, name and address of assignee, amount realized therefrom by the assignee, and disposition, of proceeds so far as known to debtor)		$
b. Property of any kind not otherwise scheduled		
	Total	

Debtor selects the following property as exempt pursuant to ☐ 11 U.S.C. §522(d)
☐ the laws of the State of..

Schedule B-4 — Property Claimed as Exempt

Type of property	Location, description, and so far as relevant to the claim of exemption, present use of property	Specify statute creating the exemption	Value claimed exempt
			$
		Total	

© 1979 JULIUS BLUMBERG, INC.

SUMMARY OF DEBTS AND PROPERTY (From the statements of the debtor in Schedule A and B)

Schedule   Total

DEBTS

A—1/a, b................Wages, etc. having priority..
A—1(c)................Deposits of money..
A—1/(d)1................Taxes owing United States..
A—1/(d)2................Taxes owing states ....
A—1 (d)3................Taxes owing other taxing authorities...
A—2................Secured claims...
A—3................Unsecured claims without priority..

                                                                     Schedule A total

PROPERTY

B—1................Real property (total value)..
B—2/a................Cash on hand..
B—2/b................Deposits ....
B—2/c................Household goods ....
B—2/d................Books, pictures, and collections...
B—2/e................Wearing apparel and personal possessions...
B—2/f................Automobiles and other vehicles..
B—2/g................Boats, motors, and accessories...
B—2/h................Livestock and other animals...
B—2/i................Farming supplies and implements..
B—2/j................Office equipment and supplies..
B—2/k................Machinery, equipment, and supplies used in business...............................
B—2/l................Inventory ....
B—2/m................Other tangible personal property..
B—2/n................Patents and other general intangibles...
B—2/o................Bonds and other instruments...
B—2/p................Other liquidated debts..
B—2/q................Contingent and unliquidated claims...
B—2/r................Interests in insurance policies...
B—2/s................Annuities ....
B—2/t................Interests in corporations and unincorporated companies............................
B—2/u................Interests in partnerships..
B—2/v................Equitable and future interests, rights, and powers in personalty................
B—3/a................Property assigned for benefit of creditors...
B—3/b................Property not otherwise scheduled...

                                                                     Schedule B total

UNSWORN DECLARATION UNDER PENALTY OF PERJURY

INDIVIDUAL(S): I(we)   and

certify under penalty of perjury that I(we) have read the foregoing schedules, consisting of   sheets, and that they are true and
correct to the best of my(our) knowledge, information, and belief.

CORPORATION: I,   the (insert president or other officer or an authorized agent)
                                                                                                        of the corporation named as debtor in this case, certify under penalty
of perjury that I have read the foregoing schedules, consisting of   sheets, and that they are true and correct to the best of my
knowledge, information, and belief.

PARTNERSHIP: I,   a (insert member or an authorized agent)
                                                                                                        of the partnership named as debtor in this case, certify under penalty
of perjury that I have read the foregoing schedules, consisting of   sheets, and that they are true and correct to the best of my
knowledge, information, and belief.

Executed on   19   ....
                                                              Signature   Signature

Form 6. Summary of debts & property, declarations.   © 1979 JULIUS BLUMBERG. INC.

BANKRUPT NAME & ADDRESS	ATTORNEY(S) NAME & ADDRESS	BANKRUPT/DEBTOR NO.
DISTRICT DIRECTOR INTERNAL REVENUE SERVICE DISTRICT OFFICE ADDRESS	START A-Z LIST OF CREDITORS	

DO NOT TYPE IN THIS AREA

If a debt is disclosed to the United States other than one for taxes, type an address for the United States Attorney for the district in which the case is pending and to the department, agent or instrumentality of the United States through which the bankrupt became indebted.

Check with your local district for addresses of state or local government agencies to which addressed label must be prepared.

© 1973 BY JULIUS BLUMBERG, INC.,

self-help law books

BUSINESS & FINANCE

How To Form Your Own California Corporation

By attorney Anthony Mancuso. Provides you with all the forms, Bylaws, Articles, minutes of meeting, stock certificates and instructions necessary to form your small profit corporation in California. It includes a thorough discussion of the practical and legal aspects of incorporation, including the tax consequences.
California Edition. $21.95

The Non-Profit Corporation Handbook

By attorney Anthony Mancuso. Completely updated to reflect all the new law changes effective January 1980. Includes all the forms, Bylaws, Articles, minutes of meeting, and instructions you need to form a nonprofit corporation in California. Step-by-step instructions on how to choose a name, draft Articles and Bylaws, attain favorable tax status. Thorough information on federal tax exemptions which groups outside of California will find particularly useful.
California Edition $21.95

The California Professional Corporation Handbook

By attorneys Mancuso and Honigsberg. In California there are a number of professions which must fulfill special requirements when forming a corporation. Among them are lawyers, dentists, doctors and other health professionals, accountants, certain social workers. This book contains detailed information on the special requirements of every profession and all the forms and instructions necessary to form a professional corporation. $21.95

Billpayers' Rights

By attorneys Honigsberg & Warner. Complete information on bankruptcy, student loans, wage attachments, dealing with bill collectors and collection agencies, credit cards, car repossessions, homesteads, child support and much more.
California Edition $10.95

The Partnership Book

By attorneys Clifford & Warner. When two or more people join to start a small business, one of the most basic needs is to establish a solid, legal partnership agreement. This book supplies a number of sample agreements with the information you will need to use them as is or to modify them to fit your needs. Buy-out clauses, unequal sharing of assets, and limited partnerships are all discussed in detail.
California Edition $15.95
National Edition $15.95

Plan Your Estate: Wills, Probate Avoidance, Trusts & Taxes

By attorney Clifford. Comprehensive information on making a will, alternatives to probate, planning to limit inheritance and estate taxes, living trusts, and providing for family and friends. An explanation of the new statutory will and usable, tear-out forms are included.
California Edition $15.95

Chapter 13: The Federal Plan To Repay Your Debts

By attorney Janice Kosel. This book allows an individual to develop and carry out a feasible plan to pay his or her debts in whole over a three-year period. Chapter 13 is an alternative to straight bankruptcy and yet it still means the end of creditor harassment, wage attachments and other collection efforts. Comes complete with all the forms and worksheets you need.
National Edition $12.95

Bankruptcy: Do-It-Yourself

By attorney Janice Kosel. Tells you exactly what bankruptcy is all about and how it affects your credit rating, your property and debts, with complete details on property you can keep under the state and federal exempt property rules. Shows you step-by-step how to do it yourself and comes with all forms and instructions necessary.
National Edition $12.95

189

Legal Care for Software

By Dan Remer. Here we show the software programmer how to protect his/her work through the use of trade secret, trademark, copyright, patent and, most especially, contractual laws and agreements. This book is full of forms and instructions that give programmers the hands-on information to do it themselves.
National Edition $24.95

We Own It!

By C.P.A.s Kamoroff and Beatty and attorney Honigsberg. This book provides the legal, tax and management information you need to start and successfully operate all types of coops and collectives. $ 9.00

FAMILY & FRIENDS

How To Do Your Own Divorce

By attorney Charles Sherman. Now in its tenth edition, this is the original "do your own law" book. It contains tear-out copies of all the court forms required for an uncontested dissolution, as well as instructions for certain special forms--military waiver, pauper's oath, lost summons, and publications of summons.
California Edition $ 9.95
Texas Edition $ 9.95

California Marriage & Divorce Law

By attorneys Ihara and Warner. This book contains invaluable information for married couples and those considering marriage on community and separate property, names, debts, children, buying a house, etc. Includes sample marriage contracts, a simple will, probate avoidance information and an explanation of gift and inheritance taxes. Discusses "secret marriage" and "common law" marriage. California Edition $14.95

How To Adopt Your Stepchild

By Frank Zagone. Shows you how to prepare all the legal forms; includes information on how to get the consent of the natural parent and how to conduct an "abandonment" proceeding. Discusses appearing in court, making changes in birth certificates.
California Edition $14.95

Small-Time Operator

By Bernard Kamoroff, C.P.A. Shows you how to start and operate your small business, keep your books, pay your taxes and stay out of trouble. Comes complete with a year's supply of ledgers and worksheets designed especially for small businesses, and contains invaluable information on permits, licenses, financing, loans, insurance, bank accounts, etc. Published by Bell Springs Press. National Edition $ 8.95

SOURCEBOOK FOR OLDER AMERICANS

By attorney Joseph Matthews. The most comprehensive resource tool on the income, rights & benefits of Americans over 55. Includes detailed information on social security, retirement rights, Medicare, Medicaid, supplemental security income, private pensions, age discrimination, as well as a thorough explanation of the new social security legislation.
National Edition $10.95

A Legal Guide for Lesbian/Gay Couples

By attorneys Hayden Curry and Denis Clifford. Here is a book that deals specifically with legal matters of lesbian and gay couples. Discusses areas such as raising children (custody, support, living with a lover), buying property together, wills, etc. and comes complete with sample contracts and agreements. National Edition $14.95

After The Divorce: How To Modify Alimony, Child Support and Child Custody

By attorney Joseph Matthews. Detailed information on how to increase alimony or child support, decrease what you pay, change custody and visitation, oppose modifications by your ex. Comes with all the forms and instructions you need. Sections on joint custody, mediation, and inflation.
California Edition $14.95

The Living Together Kit

By attorneys Ihara and Warner. A legal guide for unmarried couples with information about buying or sharing property, the Marvin decision, paternity statements, medical emergencies and tax consequences. Contains a sample will and Living Together Contract.
National Edition $14.95

The People's Law Review

Edited by Ralph Warner. This is the first compendium of people's law resources ever published. It celebrates the coming of age of the self-help law movement and contains a 50-state catalog of self-help law materials; articles on mediation and the new "non-adversary" mediation centers; information on self-help law programs and centers (programs for tenants, artists, battered women, the disabled, etc.); articles and interviews by the leaders of the self-help law movement, and articles dealing with many common legal problems which show people "how to do it themselves" without lawyers. National Edition $ 8.95

Author Law

By attorney Brad Bunnin and Peter Beren. A comprehensive explanation of the legal rights of authors. Covers contracts with publishers of books and periodicals, with sample contracts provided. Explains the legal responsibilities between co-authors and with agents, and how to do your own copyright. Discusses royalties negotiations, libel, and invasion of privacy. Includes a glossary of publishing terms. $14.95

The Criminal Records Book

By attorney Siegel. Takes you step-by-step through all the procedures available to get your records sealed, destroyed or changed. Detailed discussion on: your criminal record--what it is, how it can harm you, how to correct inaccuracies, marijuana possession records & juvenile court records. Complete with forms and instructions. $12.95

Legal Research: How To Find and Understand The Law

By attorney Steve Elias. A hands-on guide to unraveling the mysteries of the law library. For paralegals, law students, consumer activists, legal secretaries, business and media people. Shows exactly how to find laws relating to specific cases or legal questions, interpret statutes and regulations, find and research cases, understand case citations and Shepardize them. National Edition $12.95

California Tenants' Handbook

By attorneys Moskovitz, Warner & Sherman. Discusses everything tenants need to know in order to protect themselves: getting deposits returned, breaking a lease, getting repairs made, using Small Claims Court, dealing with an unscrupulous landlord, forming a tenants' organization, etc. Completely updated to cover new rent control information and law changes for 1981. Sample Fair-to-Tenants lease and rental agreements. California Edition $ 9.95

Everybody's Guide to Small Claims Court

By attorney Ralph Warner. Guides you step-by-step through the Small Claims procedure, providing practical information on how to evaluate your case, file and serve papers, prepare and present your case, and, most important, how to collect when you win. Separate chapters focus on common situations (landlord-tenant, automobile sales and repair, etc.). $ 9.95

Fight Your Ticket

By attorney David Brown. A comprehensive manual on how to fight your traffic ticket. Radar, drunk driving, preparing for court, arguing your case to a judge, cross-examining witnesses are all covered. California Edition $12.95

Homestead Your House

By attorney Warner. Under the California Homestead Act, you can file a Declaration of Homestead and thus protect your home from being sold to satisfy most debts. This book explains this simple and inexpensive procedure and includes all the forms and instructions. Contains information on exemptions for mobile homes and houseboats. California Edition $ 8.95

How To Change Your Name

By David Loeb. Changing one's name is a very simple procedure. Using this book, people can file the necessary papers themselves, saving $200-300 in attorney's fees. Comes complete with all the forms and instructions necessary for the court petition method or the simpler usage method. California Edition $14.95

...uana: Your Legal Rights

..ttorney Richard Moller. Here is the
..gal information all marijuana users
and growers need to guarantee their
constitutional rights and protect their
privacy and property. Discusses what
the laws are, how they differ from state
to state, and how legal loopholes can be
used against smokers and growers.
National Edition $9.95

The Unemployment Benefits Handbook

By attorney Peter Jan Honigsberg. Comprehensive information on how to find
out if you are eligible for benefits,
how the amount of those benefits will be
determined. It shows how to file and
handle an appeal if benefits are denied
and gives important advice on how to
deal with the bureaucracy and the people
at the unemployment office.
National Edition $ 5.95

How To Become A United States Citizen

By Sally Abel. Detailed explanation of
the naturalization process. Includes
step-by-step instructions from filing
for naturalization to the final oath of
allegiance. Includes study guide on
U.S. history & government. Text is
written in both English & Spanish. $9.95

Media Law: A Legal Handbook for the Working Journalist

By attorney Kathy Galvin. This is a
practical legal guide for the working
journalist (TV, radio and print) and
those who desire a better understanding
of how the law and journalism intersect.
It informs you about: censorship, libel
and invasion of privacy; how to gain
access to public records including
using the Freedom of Information Act;
entry to public meetings and court
rooms, and what to do about gag orders.
                                    $14.95

Murder On The Air

By Ralph Warner & Toni Ihara. An
unconventional murder mystery set in
Berkeley, California. When a noted
environmentalist and anti-nuclear
activist is killed at a local radio
station, the Berkeley violent crime
squad swings into action. James
Rivers, an unplugged lawyer, and Sara
Tamura, Berkeley's first murder squad
detective, lead the chase. The action
is fast, furious and fun. $5.95

Landlording

By Leigh Robinson. Written for the
conscientious landlord or landlady, this
comprehensive guide discusses maintenance and repairs, getting good tenants,
how to avoid evictions, recordkeeping,
and taxes. Published by Express Press.
National Edition $15.00

Write, Edit & Print

By Donald McCunn. Word processing with
personal computers. A complete how-to
manual including: evaluation of equipment, 4 fully annotated programs, oper-
ating instructions, sample application.
525 pages. $24.95

Computer Programming for The Complete Idiot

By Donald McCunn. An excellent intro-
duction to computers. Hardware and
software are explained in everyday language and the last chapter gives information on creating original programs.
                                    $6.95

Your Family Records: How to Preserve Personal, Financial and Legal Histor

By Carol Pladsen & attorney Denis
Clifford. Helps you organize and record
all sorts of items that will affect you
and your family when death or disability
occur, e.g., where to find your will and
the deed to your house. This practical
yet charming book includes information
about probate avoidance, joint ownership
of property, genealogical research, and
space is provided for financial and
legal records. $12.95

29 Reasons Not To Go To Law School

A humorous and irreverent look at the
dubious pleasures of going to law
school. By attorneys Ihara and Warner
with contributions by fellow lawyers and
illustrations by Mari Stein. $ 6.95

Order Form

QUANTITY	TITLE	UNIT PRICE	TOTAL

Prices subject to change

☐ Please send me a
catalogue of your books

Tax: (California only) 6½% for Bart,
Los Angeles, San Mateo & Santa
Clara counties; 6% for all others

Name_____

Address_____

_____

☐ I am not on Nolo's mailing list and would like to be.
(If you receive the NOLO NEWS you are on the list and
need not check the box.)

SUBTOTAL _____

Tax _____

Postage & Handling ___$1.00___

TOTAL _____

Send to:

NOLO PRESS
950 Parker St.
Berkeley, CA 94710
or

NOLO DISTRIBUTING
Box 544
Occidental, CA 95465

UPDATE SERVICE

Our books are as current as we can make them, but sometimes the laws do change between editions. You can read
about any law changes which may affect this book in the NOLO
NEWS, a 16 page newspaper which we publish quarterly.

In addition to the Update Service, each issue contains comprehensive articles about the growing self-help law movement
as well as areas of the law that are sure to affect you.

To receive the next 4 issues of the NOLO NEWS, please send us
$2.00

Name _____

Address _____

_____

Send to: NOLO PRESS, 950 Parker St., Berkeley, CA 94710

Recycle Your Out-of-Date Books & Get One
Third off your next purchase!

Using an old edition can be dangerous if information in it is wrong. This,
unfortunately, is the reality of the always-changing law. If you cut out and
deliver to us the **title portion** of the cover of **any** old Nolo book we'll give
you a 33% discount off the retail price of **any** new Nolo book. Eg., if you
have a copy of TENANTS' RIGHTS, 4th edition and want to trade it for the
latest CALIF. MARRIAGE & DIVORCE LAW, send us the TENANTS' RIGHTS cover
and a check for the current price of MARRIAGE & DIVORCE, less a 33%
discount. This is an excellent reason to subscribe to the Nolo News: you may
always find current editions and current prices listed in it (see above box).
Generally speaking, any book more than two years old is questionable.
Books more than four or five years old are a menace.

OUT OF DATE = DANGEROUS